FOREWORD

TO THE

OLD TESTAMENT BOOKS

by

FREDERICK L. MORIARTY, S.J.

Weston College Press
Weston 93, Mass.
1954

To My Father

PREFACE

THIS work is intended as an introduction to each of the Old Testament books. Although I have had uppermost in mind the needs of students at the college level, the general reader will, I trust, find it of some help in better appreciating the word which God has spoken to us in the Old Testament. There are many problems of composition, date, and authorship which still await a satisfactory solution, so the reader will often have to bear patiently with probabilities where he might be looking for clearcut certainty.

Nevertheless, the rediscovery of the biblical world in our own lifetime has brought us a better understanding of the biblical message, and the unremitting labors of many devoted scholars have led to a deeper appreciation of these inspired records. Many difficulties remain but they should not obscure the real and lasting progress achieved in our improved theological and historical understanding of the Old Testament. The positions held in this work on controverted questions have the backing of one or several recognized authorities in the world of scholarship but I have not thought it advisable to cite names in each case. My indebtedness to others will be obvious to those who are working in the field. Wherever possible I have used the new and excellent translation of the Old Testament which is published under the auspices of the Confraternity of Christian Doctrine. In other places the translation is my own. The spelling of proper names is based upon the original text, marking a departure from the standardized *Vulgate forms with which the student is perhaps more familiar.

It may be that certain names and places will be unfamiliar to the general reader. An asterisk, placed at the first occurrence of the word, refers to the Glossary at the end of the book and there the student will find a brief explanation. One who reads the Old Testament soon learns that not all passages or sections are of equal importance or interest. For this reason I have occasionally added to the introduction of a book a list of suggested readings which deserve the special attention of the reader. It cannot be sufficiently emphasized that this selection in no way implies that the rest may be passed over. The goal of this book is to help the student read the *entire* Old Testament. It is a pleasant duty to thank the Rev. William J. Casey, S.J., Chairman of the Department of Theology at Boston College, for his never-failing assistance and many helpful suggestions. The maps are due to the skill and good taste of the Rev. Leo J. McDonough, S.J. of Weston College.

CONTENTS

IMPORTANT DATES IN THE BIBLICAL WORLD

Hebrew History	B. C.	Ancient Near East
Abraham	1900?	End of Third Dynasty of Ur—1950
Joseph in Egypt	1720	Hyksos Invasion of Egypt
		Babylon under King Hammurabi
Moses, and Exodus from Egypt	1290	Ramses II, Pharaoh of the Exodus
Joshua, and Fall of Jericho	1219	*Stele of Mer-Ne-Ptah
Philistines in Land of Canaan	1200	Trojan War
Saul (1020) ascends throne.		
David (1000) ascends throne.	1000	Homer
Solomon (961) ascends throne.		
Division of the Kingdom	922	Pharaoh Shishak's Invasion of Palestine (919)

Judah	Israel		
	Elijah		Carthage founded (800)
	Elisha		
	Amos, Hosea	750	*Assyria:*
Isaiah			Tiglath Pileser III (744)
Micah			
	Fall of Samaria	721	Sargon II (722)
Kingdom of Judah			Sennacherib (704)
Jeremiah			
Sophoniah		612	Fall of Nineveh
Nahum			
Death of King Josiah (609)			
First Siege of Jerusalem	597	*Babylon:*
Ezekiel in Babylonia		Nebuchadnezzar
Fall of Jerusalem	587	
Beginning of the Exile		
Restoration of the Jews (538)	538	*Persia:*
		Cyrus conquers Babylon (539)
Zerubbabel		Edict of Cyrus (538)
Haggai		
Zechariah		
Dedication of Second Temple	515	
Ezra and Nehemiah	450	
Malachi		
		Greece:
	333	Conquest of Persia by Alexander the Great
Desecration of the Temple (167)	175	Antiochus Epiphanes
Revolt of Maccabees		
		Rome:
Jerusalem falls to Pompey	63	Pompey intervenes in Syria
Birth of Christ	7	

INTRODUCTION

THE Old Testament is the inspired record of God's ways with the People of Israel. Though it grew out of the history of that one community and was written by the descendants of Abraham, it is also, for the Christian, a cherished part of his Sacred Writings. Catholics have always recognized a divinely guided continuity between the Old and the New Testaments, to the extent that one cannot be understood without the other. The *Covenant made with Abraham has prepared the way for the New Covenant of Christ, just as the kingship of David prefigured the kingship of Christ. For this and other reasons the Church has always esteemed the Old Testament as a sacred heritage, defended it against heretics like *Marcion who rejected it, and incorporated large parts of it in her public worship of God. It suffices to recall the central place occupied by the Psalms in the Roman Breviary.

Before taking up the books individually it will be useful to note some of the larger divisions of the Old Testament. According to the Jewish *Canon, which is prior in time to all others, we have the following threefold division of the Old Testament.

1. The *Law*, or *Torah*, comprising the first five books of the Bible, and sometimes referred to as the "Pentateuch". These books are *Genesis, Exodus, Leviticus, Numbers,* and *Deuteronomy.*

2. The *Prophets*, divided into the "Former Prophets" (*Joshua, Judges,* the two *Books of Samuel* and the two *Books of Kings*) and the "Latter Prophets" (*Isaiah, Jeremiah, Ezekiel,* and the *Twelve Minor Prophets*). Though many of these books are strictly historical writings, early Jewish tradition attributed their composition to prophets.

1

3. The *Writings,* which include several books, among them the *Psalms, Proverbs,* and *Job.* These are followed in the Canon by the "Five Rolls", five short books arranged according to the great feasts of the Jewish Calendar. On each of these feasts one of the books is read in the synagogue service. These books are the *Song of Songs* (*Passover), *Ruth* (*Feast of Weeks), *Lamentations* (read on the 9th of *Ab, which commemorates the two destructions of Jerusalem, in 587 B.C. and 70 A.D.), *Ecclesiastes* (*Feast of Booths or Tabernacles) and *Esther* (*Feast of Purim). The Writings conclude with *Daniel, Ezra-Nehemiah,* and the two *Books of Chronicles,* or *Paralipomenon.*

This collection of sacred writings, known as the *Palestinian Canon, may have been officially promulgated as early as the second century before Christ though its origins go back much earlier. In any case, it was solemnly fixed for succeeding ages in the Jewish community at the Council of Jamnia, around 90 A.D., twenty years after Jerusalem was destroyed by the Romans. All of the books in the Palestinian Canon were written in the Hebrew language, with a few insertions in *Aramaic. Our Lord referred to this Canon when He said: "On these two commandments depend the whole Law and the Prophets." (*Matt.* 22:40)

Along with the Palestinian Canon there existed in the pre-Christian era the *Canon of Alexandria. This famous Egyptian metropolis was the center of a thriving Jewish community in the period known as the *Diaspora, or Dispersion. The Alexandrian Canon contained more sacred books than the Palestinian because works composed in Greek, the only language known by many Jews in Egypt, were admitted to this list of sacred writings along with all the others already found in the Palestinian Canon. The

Catholic canonical books of *Tobias, Judith, Wisdom, Baruch,* the *Letter of Jeremiah, Ecclesiasticus, First* and *Second Maccabees,* and certain additions to *Daniel* and *Esther,* belong to this collection. In passing, it may be noted that *Ecclesiasticus* and *First Maccabees* are Greek translations of Hebrew originals. The Catholic Church holds all of these books to be sacred and canonical and thus approves the Alexandrian Canon of Scripture. After the Reformation the Protestants, not without some hesitation, decided to admit only those books found in the Palestinian Canon. This accounts for one of the important differences between Protestant and Catholic bibles.

Catholics divide the Old Testament in the following manner:

1. HISTORICAL BOOKS: *Genesis, Exodus, Leviticus, Numbers, Deuteronomy, Joshua, Judges,* the four *Books of Kings,* the two *Books* of *Paralipomenon* (Chronicles), *Ezra-Nehemiah, Tobias, Judith, Esther,* and the two *Books of Maccabees.*

2. *SAPIENTIAL BOOKS: Job, Psalms, Proverbs, Ecclesiastes, Song of Songs, Book of Wisdom, Ecclesiasticus.*

3. PROPHETIC BOOKS: *Isaiah, Jeremiah* (to which are added *Lamentations* and *Baruch*), *Ezekiel, Daniel,* the *Twelve Minor Prophets.*

It is important to note that in our discussion of the individual books of the Old Testament we shall follow the order:

1. HISTORICAL BOOKS
2. PROPHETIC BOOKS
3. SAPIENTIAL BOOKS

* * * * * *

The student must, at the outset, realize that the Bible is not a single, unified literary piece, but a library of books in which every style and type of writing is represented. It is extremely important to recognize this fact when interpreting individual texts or entire books. For there is hardly a form or category of literature which is not found in the Old Testament. Among these literary forms we find:

Epic fragments (the narrative of Joseph and his brothers).

Short Story (*Ruth* and *Esther*).

Historical narrative in the strict sense (History of David in *II Samuel*).

Legislative texts (the Mosaic Code in *Exodus* 20-23).

Genealogical Lists (descendants of Sem in *Gen.* 11:10 ff.).

Speeches of Reproach (the beginning of the prophecy of Amos).

Prophecies of benediction and curse (*Deut.* 28).

Prayers (the *Psalms*).

Love-poetry (the *Song of Songs*).

Prophetic oracles (*Isaiah* 7).

Letters (Edict of Nebuchadnezzar, *Dan.* 3:31 ff.).

Since the exegete's task is to determine exactly what the author intended to say in any given passage, it is clear how important is the study of these literary forms, or categories of literature. The truth in a scientific historical narrative, for example, is expressed in quite a different way from the truth in a lyric poem. Both a textbook in Algebra and *Alice in Wonderland* have truth to communicate, but not in the same way. Since the Old Testament contains such a rich variety of literary forms, many of which are peculiar to the ancient oriental world, the student must take into careful consideration the character of these forms under penalty of misinterpreting their message. To cite but one example, the first eleven chapters of *Genesis* present great difficulties to the interpreter precisely because of the strange and often unfamiliar literary forms which the author has used as the vehicle of his thought. On this point the *Biblical Commission, in its Letter to the late Cardinal Suhard (Jan. 16, 1948) remarked as follows:

"The literary forms of the first eleven chapters of *Genesis* do not correspond to any of our classical categories and cannot be judged in the light of Greco-Latin or modern literary types. It is therefore impossible to deny or to affirm their historicity as a whole, without unduly applying to them norms of a literary type under which they cannot be classed."

Nor should these literary forms or categories be determined and understood independently of other ancient Semitic literary compositions. As our knowledge of the literature of the Near East continues to be appreciably broadened by contact with an ever-increasing flow of this new material, we will be in a better position to judge the literary forms of the Old Testament and hence the precise message or truth which the author sought to convey. The word of God is expressed in the language of man. In the case of the Old Testament, the man was a native of the Near East and the heir of a rich cultural tradition. The recovery of that ancient civilization, and especially its literature, is one of the great achievements of our time and it has afforded an indispensable means of better understanding the Old Testament.

THE HISTORICAL BOOKS

The Pentateuch: The first five books of the Bible come under this title (from the Greek word *pentateuchos*, consisting of five books) which designates a five-volume work. Broadly looked at, the Pentateuch is a biblical account of the world, from Creation to the death of Moses. All scholars now admit that it is basically historical, even though parts of it are not history in the modern sense of the word. Because of its clear theological purpose, which stands out on every page, some prefer to speak of the Pentateuch as "sacred history". A long Jewish and Christian tradition attributes the authorship of this vast work to Moses, without asserting that Moses has personally written every part of the five books. Take just the matter of law. It is to be expected that, in any historical community, new civil and religious laws will be needed to meet new conditions of life. While Moses undoubtedly laid down the basic principles of Hebrew law, common sense tells us that any body of laws and customs undergoes normal development in a living group or nation. We have a parallel to this in the history of our own U.S. Constitution and its Amendments.

Another feature of the Pentateuch deserves our attention. As it exists today in our Hebrew Bible, the Pentateuch seems to be the result of a long literary and oral transmission from one generation to the next. Some of these narratives, poems, and stories would be handed down in writing, others by word of mouth. By this twofold method, for which parallels exist in the ancient and even the modern Near East, ancient material was transmitted from one period to another within the historical community of Israel. Complex as the history of that transmission may be, we are certain that the contents go back in substance to that critical period of Israel's formation in which the central figure is the great Lawgiver, Moses.

Along with the question of Mosaic authorship is the problem of sources or documents which have gone into the makeup of the Pentateuch. The Biblical Commission, in the same Letter of Jan. 16, 1948, offered some wholesome advice on this point. It reminded us that, today, there are scholars who, quite apart from religious considerations, have seriously challenged the rigid documentary theories which were in vogue fifty years ago. At that time the neat analysis of the Pentateuch into literary documents and sub-documents was generally accepted as one of the assured results of biblical criticism.

But the certitudes of one generation have turned out to be the problems of the next. No longer can the student be content with a purely literary approach to the problem. A new way of tackling the problem of the Pentateuch seeks to explain many of its peculiarities and variations of style, not so much from an alleged diversity of written documents, as in the special psychology and literary processes of the ancient oriental writer. As noted above, the importance of oral tradition among the people of the Near East has finally won deserved recognition as an important means of handing down prose and poetry. We live in the twentieth century and in a world where books are a commonplace. But, in antiquity, the pupil was expected to memorize his Homer and Vergil and, even in our own day, some students of the Bible have been known to memorize the entire Old Testament! The more we learn about these ancient processes of handing down compositions by word of mouth, the more likely are we to find a key to some of these important problems in the Pentateuch.

Although realizing that the Pentateuchal question still needs further study, a few tentative observations may be made about the origin and formation of this great work. What we propose is only probable insofar as we are dealing with a problem which still resists a solution acceptable to all, or even to the majority. Beyond the admission that various sources have been combined and woven together in the Pentateuch as we have it today, there is little agreement as to date, number, or nature of the sources or the way in which they have been brought together in their final form. What a sharp contrast between the present uncertainty and the assurance which existed among scholars of an earlier generation! At that time, the enthusiastic followers of *Wellhausen were celebrating the definitive triumph of his neat, evolutionistic division of the Pentateuch into four dated documents which reflected four progressive stages in the religious growth of Israel.

We have already seen that, today, all is changed, and new approaches to the problem, especially from the standpoint of oral tradition, have reopened the whole question of the formation of the Pentateuch. This does not mean that Wellhausen and the theory he popularized were all wrong, much less that we can neglect the long and patient critical work which non-Catholics have devoted to this vexing problem. When the Biblical Commission, in 1906, issued its Decree on the Mosaic Authorship of the Pentateuch, its purpose was to warn Catholic exegetes against certain extreme and now discredited views of the Wellhausen School. But the Decree did not call a halt to further investigation on the part of Catholics nor a retreat to fixed positions.

Many Catholic scholars are now inclined to see in the

Pentateuch a combination of traditions or cycles of traditions, each of which has its distinguishing characteristics. To speak of these sources as written documents is perhaps too mechanical, especially in view of what has been said about the importance of oral transmission in the ancient Near East. The complexity of the process and our distance in time from it are bound to leave us with a large margin of uncertainty. Allowing for the fact that the precise number of these sources is still uncertain, we can briefly enumerate and describe four of these tradition-complexes or cycles which have gone into the formation of the Pentateuch.

1. The *Yahwist Tradition*, so called because of its partiality to "Yahweh" as the divine name. The narratives making up this tradition are more primitive and archaic in style, colorful, epic in character, more concrete, and endowed with a certain dramatic intensity. To this Tradition belong the older of the two creation accounts (*Gen.* 2:4b-25), the narrative of the Fall of Adam and Eve, the story of Sodom and Gomorrha, much of the patriarchal history, and some of the most vivid incidents in the life of Moses, such as the slaying of the brutal Egyptian taskmaster (*Exodus* 2:11-23) and the impressive renewal of the Covenant made between Yahweh and His people (*Exodus* 34:1-28). The Yahwist Tradition is generally associated with the Kingdom of Judah as the place of its origin and development.

2. The *Elohist Tradition* prefers "Elohim" as the name for God. The "Elohim" sections are more sober in their style, less vivacious than the Yahwist Tradition. For example, this Tradition avoids describing God in human fashion

(anthropomorphism), that is, speaking of the "face of God" or the "breath of His anger" or "His outstretched arm". It is more precise in its terminology, and its language is more consciously artistic. In all likelihood this Tradition originated and flourished in Northern Israel. After the fall of North Israel's capital, Samaria, in 721, the Tradition was brought to Judah where it was joined to the Yahwist Tradition.

3. The *Sacerdotal Tradition* is concerned with the ritual laws of the Hebrews regarding the sanctuary, religious feasts, and various sacrifices. In a word, its spirit is juridical and institutional, reflecting the spirit and preoccupations of the priesthood which goes back to Aaron, the brother of Moses. The creation account at the very beginning of *Genesis,* which serves as a magnificent overture to the entire Old Testament, is a good example of this Tradition. Even in this majestic narrative the liturgical and, in a sense, the legal spirit, stands out. In its final *redaction, the Sacerdotal Tradition belongs to the *post-Exilic period, though a large part of its material goes back to a much earlier date. The entire *Book of Leviticus* belongs to this Tradition.

4. The *Deuteronomic Tradition* in the Pentateuch is most apparent in the Book which bears this name. It emphasizes a theology of history centering about the love of Yahweh for Israel and the loving obedience which Yahweh demands from His people. Israel is the special object of His choice; she receives Palestine as her inheritance. If Israel is faithful to Yahweh she will be blessed; infidelity shall bring speedy retribution.

"Now, Israel, hear the statutes and decrees which I (Moses) am teaching you to observe, that you may live,

and may enter in and take possession of the land which the Lord, the God of your fathers, is giving you." (DEUT. 4:1.)

We have in this Tradition the statement of a divine pedagogy by which Israel is taught not only that Yahweh demands obedience but that the only obedience worthy of the name is one which springs from love and gratitude. This teaching, or spirit, has animated the subsequent books of *Joshua, Judges,* and *Kings,* giving a profound unity to this great historical work which recounts the great deeds which Yahweh did for His people. Even if we grant that the book of *Deuteronomy* has some relation to the Reform of the pious King Josiah in 621 B.C., it is still undeniable that the ancient traditions embodied in this work go back centuries before this Reform.

Despite the differences in style, view-point, and subject matter, it would be a serious mistake to overlook the basic unity in these four cycles or Traditions. All four go back ultimately to that period in which Israel was formed as a nation, and that epoch is dominated by one outstanding personality—Moses. He not only led his people out of the bondage of Egypt; he was also their lawgiver and religious teacher. Later adaptations to their new circumstances in the Land of Canaan were made in the spirit of the norms which Moses had already laid down. We are obliged to recognize, as Israelite tradition consistently asserts, the preponderant part played by Moses in the total formation of the people of Israel and its age-old traditions. In this sense we are thoroughly justified in speaking of the Mosaic authorship of the Pentateuch. It is now time to consider the books individually.

GENESIS:

Genesis, or the book of origins, is a profoundly religious work which embodies some of the oldest traditions of the Hebrew people. The Book can be divided into two unequal parts:

I.   Primitive History, which includes, in chapters one to eleven: (a) the Creation and Fall of Man; (b) the Deluge; (c) from the Deluge to Abraham.

II.   Patriarchal History, which includes, in chapters twelve to fifty, the histories of Abraham, Isaac, Jacob, and Joseph.

The ancient traditions contained in the first eleven chapters have, in all likelihood, been brought from Mesopotamia, the ancestral home of the Hebrews. But whatever may have been their origin, these traditions are now the picturesque and colorful vehicle of theological doctrine which is unique in the ancient world. The creation narratives, for example, of the first two chapters, through an imagery in keeping with oriental modes of expression, reveal the purest monotheistic doctrine of the one, eternal God, creator of heaven and earth. This creation, through the power of God's word, is due solely to the divine goodness which seeks to communicate itself to creatures. "God saw that it was good" is the refrain running through the majestic creation account. In striking contrast to the brooding pessimism which darkens so many pages of pagan literature, there is a wholesome optimism in the narratives of the Old Testament. For the Hebrew, the whole world came fresh from the hand of a loving God. Come what may, death, famine, persecution, or even national calamity, however dark the future might appear, Israel held tenaciously to her basic conviction that the world was good and that it was permeated through and through with its divine origin and high purpose.

At the summit of creation is man, drawn from the dust of the earth, and yet made in the image and likeness of God. This union of the divine with the earthly helps us to understand both the glory and the tragedy of man in his pilgrimage through history. God gave man a supernatural destiny, to live in friendship with Him. But God has also given him a free will by which he can spurn His gifts. Tempted and deceived by the Enemy of human nature, our first parents sinned, transgressing a divine command of a serious nature. Original sin entered the world, with all its consequences. Yet God tempered His sentence of condemnation by a mysterious promise of future salvation.

> *"I will put enmity between you and the woman,*
> *between your seed and her seed;*
> *He shall crush your head,*
> *and you shall lie in wait for his heel."* (GEN. 3:15)

This verse has been called the *protoevangelium,* or the first good-tidings of our salvation through Christ. The process of reconciliation and of restoration to our lost inheritance had begun.

Following hard upon the crime of Cain, who acted out of jealousy, corruption became so widespread that God sent the Deluge as a punishment. After the Flood a covenant was drawn up between God and Noah, who represented mankind; it was another step in God's plan to restore man to His friendship. The survivors of the Flood would be required to prove their fidelity to God by observance of His divine commands. The biblical account of the Tower of Babel (*Gen. 9:1-7*), for which

Mesopotamian parallels exist, along with the confusion of tongues, gives us God's answer to a nation's inordinate pride and self-sufficiency. We should note how *Genesis*, in a few chapters, has portrayed sin and divine judgment at every level of human life. With Adam and Eve it is a question of sin in the individual; the Cain and Abel episode shows us the work of sin in the family; the Flood narrative concerns sin and its consequences in society; and the Tower of Babel dramatizes the confusion resulting from sinful pride on the national level. Primitive history closes with the genealogy of Sem, bringing us to the birth of Abraham and the beginning of patriarchal history.

Summoned from a land of many gods by the one true God, Abraham journeyed from Haran, in Mesopotamia, to the land of Canaan. There, in virtue of a covenant with Yahweh, Abraham became the ancestor of a chosen people. This covenant was to be solemnly renewed and promulgated on Sinai by Moses, more than five hundred years later. Abraham's faith was tested by his willingness to sacrifice his only son, Isaac. The passing of the test won for Abraham that great title "Father of the faithful". The biographies of Isaac, Jacob, and Joseph follow in that order, each throwing some new light on life in patriarchal days. It is possible to find a dominant theme or religious lesson in some of these life-histories. Abraham is the model of a faith which has been tried and rewarded; Jacob's good fortune illustrates the freedom of the divine choice, independent of the merits of the person (*Romans* 9:13). In the life of Joseph a divine Providence is discernible which knows how to turn all things, even the misdeeds of men, to its own purposes. As Joseph says to his brothers: "You intended evil against me, but God intended it for good, to do as He has done today, namely, to save the lives of many people." (*Gen.* 50:20)

It would be unfair to judge the patriarchal history according to the standards of modern historical writing. History in *Genesis* is written in the popular, anecdotal style proper to the ancient Near East; unlike most of our modern history, it is written from a profoundly religious viewpoint, seeking to find in every event the directing hand of God. In the story of the patriarchs incidents are selected, facts are explained, with a view to showing God's plan of choosing and forming one people and settling it in the land of His choice. Nevertheless, the patriarchal narrative is truly historical in that it records, in its own popular way, real events, centering around real persons who lived in the early centuries of the second millennium before Christ. By long and patient work, archaeologists and historians of the ancient Near East have revolutionized our knowledge of the patriarchal Age and given us a truer appreciation of the trustworthiness of Hebrew tradition. The scientific unearthing of great Mesopotamian sites such as *Nuzu, *Mari on the Euphrates, and *Nippur in ancient *Sumer, has afforded us a new and often brilliant picture of the international culture which flourished in that Age. Although much has been accomplished, we may be sure that new and exciting discoveries lie ahead which will round out our picture of the patriarchal age. Now that we can see more clearly the life of the patriarchs within the social, economic and legal framework of the contemporary Near East, skepticism about the historical reliability of our narrative is unwarranted and has been abandoned by all who are acquainted with the rediscovery of the biblical world in the last fifty years.

Note: The student should read the entire book of *Genesis* because of its important religious teaching about God and man. The beginnings of God's redemptive plan and the first steps towards its achievement are described in this Book.

EXODUS:

The second Book of the Pentateuch develops two major themes: the deliverance of the children of Israel from the bondage of Egypt, and the solemn promulgation of the Covenant at Mt. Sinai. The first fifteen chapters tell of the providential deliverance from Egypt. The descendants of Jacob had settled in Goshen, a part of the fertile Nile Delta, and had increased in numbers at a rate which alarmed the Egyptians. A hostile Pharaoh not only oppressed them cruelly but even planned to exterminate them. From this time, around 1300 B.C., Egypt became the symbol of the oppressor of God's people, and the power of this world which seeks to thwart the designs of God. But God was mindful of His promises to the patriarchs. He called Moses from the flocks of Jethro and appeared to him from out the burning bush. God then revealed to Moses the sacred name, Yahweh ("He who is" or "He who causes to exist") and commissioned him to lead His people out of slavery. A series of plagues finally broke down the obstinacy of the Pharaoh (probably *Ramses II), and the Israelites set out on the long journey which was to bring them into the land of Canaan. The first celebration of the Passover was built around the slain lamb which saved the Hebrews from the Angel of Death. The memory of that momentous event in their history has never been absent from the children of Israel. From that time, the recollection that an angry Yahweh did not strike down their first-born but, instead, delivered them from their persecutors, has been stamped upon the great annual Passover festival whose very rite served as a solemn reminder that Israel had been redeemed by the Lord.

"When your children ask you, 'What does this rite of yours mean?', you shall reply, 'This is the Passover sacrifice of the Lord, Who passed over the houses of the Israelites in Egypt; when He struck down the Egyptians, He spared our houses'." (EXODUS 12:27)

To every pious Jew, the celebration of the Feast recalls the days when their fathers, loins girt and staff in hand, ate the first paschal lamb, the bitter herbs and the unleavened bread—when the God of Israel proved mightier than all the gods of Egypt.

The Feast has become the type of our Christian Pasch in which the Lamb of God is slain to deliver us from the death of sin. In the beautiful Easter liturgy the Church sings in the Epistle of the Mass the words of St. Paul:

"Christ, our Passover, has been sacrificed. Therefore let us keep festival, not with the old leaven, nor with the leaven of malice and wickedness, but with the unleavened bread of sincerity and truth." (FIRST CORINTHIANS 5:8)

Once in the Desert, God gathered the people together at the foot of Mt. Sinai and sealed His election of Israel with a solemn Covenant. Israel proclaimed that Yahweh was her only God and that she would serve no other but Him; Yahweh, in turn, would treat Israel as His people and would protect her from her enemies as long as she remained faithful. The Ten Commandments and the longer Code of the Covenant contained the terms of this alliance which was ratified in a most impressive scene— God's appearance on the summit of Mt. Sinai. This appearance (often called a "theophany" or appearance of

God), made such a lasting impression that subsequent writers, whether prophets or psalmists, would use the theophany of Sinai as their model in describing any solemn coming of Yahweh, especially if He came in judgment.

The Code of the Covenant, which is extremely ancient in its nucleus, was a first draft of that social and religious legislation which would serve as the basis for all later ordinances. The Covenant was solemnly concluded with a sacrifice.

"Taking the Book of the Covenant, he (Moses) read it aloud to the people, who answered, 'All that the Lord has said we will heed and do.' Then he took the blood and sprinkled it on the people, saying, 'This is the blood of the Covenant which the Lord has made with you in accordance with all these words of his'." (EXODUS 24:7-8)

Hardly had universal assent been given to this pact with Yahweh when Israel fell into idolatry at the very foot of the Mountain. Despite the divine wrath, Yahweh listened to the intercession of Moses and the Covenant was renewed and the Commandments reiterated. The final chapters (35-40) describe the construction of the Tabernacle and its furnishings. The Ark of the Covenant became the visible symbol of God's dwelling with His people, and a pledge that He would be faithful to His promises. In any Catholic Church, the Tabernacle, which is often modelled after the Ark of the Covenant, should remind us that God still dwells with His people, but now in a far more perfect manner. God's dwelling among His people in the Old Testament was a preparation for a great Mystery because the Eucharistic Presence is the perfect fulfillment of God's promise to live always with man. As the priest of the New Law mounts the steps of the altar each morning, he approaches not merely the place of sacrifice, but the dwelling of the Son of God, of whom St. John says:

> And the Word was made flesh,
>   and dwelt among us.
> And we saw his glory,
>   glory as of the only-begotten of the father,
>   full of grace and of truth. (JOHN 1:14)

[*Suggested readings:*]

Chapters 1 to 15: The deliverance from Egypt.

Chapters 20 to 23: The Ten Commandments and the Book of the Covenant.

Chapter 34: Renewal of the Covenant after the lapse into idolatry.

LEVITICUS:

The third Book of the Pentateuch takes its name from its preoccupation with the duties of the family of Levi and his descendants. The first seven chapters contain a detailed and somewhat tedious account of the various sacrifices to be offered by the Israelites. We may group these sacrifices under the following categories:

1. The Holocaust, or Burnt Offering, in which the victim is wholly consumed in the fire. It seems to have been a very ancient form of sacrifice in Israel.

2. The Peace Offering, sometimes called a "Communion Sacrifice" because it was accompanied by a sacred banquet. This type of sacrifice was common among Semitic peoples.

3. The Cereal Offering, proper to a sedentary people engaged in agriculture.

4. The Sin Offering, attached to the commission of some fault, even though it be only involuntary. The fault might be against a person or merely a violation of some ritual prescription.

There are no grounds for holding, as some have in the

past, that the Hebrew sacrificial system was nothing but a purely external, mechanical set of observances which were denounced by the prophets and in which God took no pleasure. The prophets denounced abuses, mere externalism, but not sacrifice itself, which the Mosaic Law prescribed. When the offering came from a heart which was contrite and eager to acknowledge God's supreme dominion, it was a meritorious and meaningful action. In the fullness of time the Sacrifice of the New Law, centered in the Person of Christ, would render obsolete all these preparatory institutions which have, in some way, prefigured the sacrifice of the only-begotten Son. We should note that the Sacrifice of the Mass, rich in its Old Testament overtones, fulfills in a perfect manner the various purposes of Levitical sacrifices.

Long sections of *Leviticus* are devoted to legal purity and many of the precepts of this sacerdotal work are still observed by Orthodox Jews today. The Hebrews made the observance of these prescriptions, that is, the avoidance of contact with anything legally "unclean" a necessary condition for partaking in the social and ceremonial life of the people. The concept of a holy, "clean" community is one of the essential ideas underlying this legislation. The same idea of a holy congregation, set apart from the nations by the will of Yahweh, prepared the way for that one, holy Church which is called the Spouse of Christ. This Church marks the realization of a long Old Testament preparation, which has left its imprint even on the most solemn act of worship in the New Law.

[*Suggested readings:*]

Chapters 17 to 26: This section is known as the Holiness Code and is a well-rounded body of law regulating both liturgy and general moral conduct.

NUMBERS:

The fourth Book of the Pentateuch has an arithmetical quality which accounts for both its title and its peculiar character. There is, for example, the two-fold census, the first (chapter 1) in the Desert of Sinai, and the second (chapter 26) on the plains of Moab. But a careful reader will also notice the attention consistently given to numerical quantities, whether it is a question of the princely offerings, or the exact measuring of the sacrificial oblations and libations, or the division of booty taken on the battlefield, or the amount of territory granted to a Levitic city. All of these statistical regulations give a special coloring to this Book, which aims at the building of an ordered community destined to live under the laws of God in the Promised Land.

But this community was not a disembodied society, a purely spiritual unit unconcerned with the practicalities of everyday life. No, this society moved across the wild and uninhabitable Peninsula of Sinai, lived off the land as best it could, struggled against enemies both within and without. The old traditions incorporated in *Numbers* afford a glimpse of these bitter feuds and the battles which Israel had to fight before it could take possession of its inheritance. Edomites, Moabites, Amalekites, Kenites, and Ammonites appear in these historical records which take up where the *Exodus* narrative ended and bring us up to the eve of Conquest. The work is composite in its structure and contains material from different periods of Israelite history. Further legislation, both civil and religious, has been added as new conditions warranted.

Numbers, like the other books of the Pentateuch, is primarily a theological work built upon elements which are authentically historical. But the historical event is not, as in modern historical writing, narrated for its own sake. History here serves, above all, to better our knowledge of God and of His working in history. The solid historical foundation, in this case, is supplied by the old and trust-worthy traditions, especially those connected with the sojourn at Kadesh and those which describe the preliminary contacts with other nations. One who understands the moral and religious evils to which the Hebrews were ex-posed by such contacts will be in a better position to judge the drastic measures taken then and later by the people of Israel. Assimilation would have been fatal as far as the religion of Yahweh was concerned.

Thanks to the archaeologist, linguist, and historian, the whole picture of this important transitional period in the history of Israel can now be seen in clearer perspective. There is, for example, the problem of the 33rd chapter of *Numbers* which narrates the stages on the journey out of Egypt. Many years ago it was fashionable to treat this list of forty stations as late and unreliable. Now, in the light of our new knowledge, the route appears most logical and in perfect accord with conditions which prevailed in Egypt of the Eighteenth and Nineteenth Dynasties. Avoid-ing the well-travelled and strongly fortified route to Pales-tine, the Israelites headed south toward the mining region of Sinai. The noted Dominican scholar, Father Abel, has identified Dephkah (verse 13) with the prosperous Egyptian mining center of Serabit el-Khadem, while an American archaeologist, Nelson Glueck, has brilliantly excavated and reported the great copper-smelting center of Ezion-Geber, which is mentioned in verse 35. Census lists, another feature of the Book, have turned up at the excavated sites of *Mari and *Ugarit, attesting to the antiquity of such practices in the ancient world. In countless ways such as this, auxiliary sciences have come to our aid in confirming the substantial reliability of the ancient traditions preserved in the Pentateuch.

By far the most colorful episode in the narrative portion of *Numbers* is the story of Balaam, the north Syrian diviner who is hired to curse Israel, but can only bless her.

"From Aram has Balac brought me,
Moab's king from the Eastern Mountains:
'Go you and curse for me Jacob,
Go and denounce Israel.'
How can I curse whom God has not cursed?
How can I denounce whom Yahweh has not denounced?"

(NUMBERS 23:7-8)

In such unforgettable lines as these, and elsewhere in the poems of Balaam, we have some of the oldest poetry in the Old Testament. The rough vigor of this archaic literature admirably reflects the atmosphere of the age in which it was composed. In passing we might also note that the Balaam event provides us with one of the earliest examples of prophetic ecstasy.

The inspired authors of the New Testament have seen in *Numbers* many incidents or things which foreshadow realities in the New Testament. These incidents, or persons, or things, which are found in the Old Testament are known as "types" and the science which discovers and explains these types is called *"typology", a favorite method of interpretation among the early Fathers of the Church. The student should note that the existence of a true type can be known only from revelation. It is God Who determines that this person, thing, or event shall stand as a type of a future and greater reality. To take *Numbers* alone, the bronze serpent, the rebellion of Core, the Manna, the fidelity of Moses, and the rock from which Israel drank, are realities which, through God's design, have assumed a new and deeper significance in the New Testament.

[*Suggested readings:*]

Chapters 11 to 14: Events during the forty years of wandering in the wilderness.

Chapters 16 and 17: Rebellion against Moses, and the incident of Aaron's rod.

Chapters 20 to 24: Journey from Kadesh to the plains of Moab. The oracles of Balaam.

DEUTERONOMY:

The name of the last Book of the Pentateuch means "the second law"; it repeats and amplifies legislation already promulgated in the previous books. More precisely, chapters 12 to 26, the strictly juridical part of *Deuteronomy*, contain an expanded version of the Law as found in chapters 20 to 23 of *Exodus*. But the author is no mere collector of laws; he expounds them by describing the moral purposes which they subserve, and the motives which should prompt Israelite obedience to them. Aside from the purely legal matters, hortatory discourses in the oratorical style play a very important part in this work. By many, *Deuteronomy* is considered the supreme example of sacred history as understood by the Hebrews. The limpid prose of the Book marks the high point of classical Hebrew style, and embodies some of the most eloquent oratory in the Old Testament. Though the Book is a compilation of legal, oratorical, and narrative materials, the following outline may be given:

1. Introductory Discourses: chapters 1 to 11.
2. The Deuteronomic Code: chapters 12 to 26.
3. Concluding Discourses: chapters 27 to 30.
4. Last Days of Moses, including, (a) Canticle of Moses: chapter 32; (b) Blessing of Moses: chapter 33; (c) Death of Moses: chapter 34.

However complex the structure of *Deuteronomy* may appear, it finds its unity in the profoundly religious spirit which pervades the entire work. The author wrote with a keen sense of the perils of idolatry, to which Israel was so prone, and he saw in that sin an act of ingratitude towards its sovereign God Who had intervened time and again in the crises of its history. The author felt an all-absorbing sense of personal devotion to God, and his ideal Israelite was the man who was ready to renounce anything inconsistent with the will of Yahweh. The great Deuteronomic theme of proportion between fidelity and blessings runs throughout. "Thus, then, shall it be: if you continue to heed the voice of the Lord, your God, and are careful to observe all His commandments which I enjoin on you today, the Lord, your God, will raise you high above all the nations of the earth." (*Deut.* 28:1) With these words Moses solemnly pronounced the blessings promised to those who obey Yahweh, followed by the terrible curses reserved for those who violate the Covenant.

Biblical criticism has not yet reached a satisfactory solution to the problem of the composition and date of *Deuteronomy*. It is very likely that the Book is the product of a long oral and written transmission and was edited in successive stages. It is possible that the last edition was made some time after the Exile, but all of these views on the origin of the work are subject to further revision.

Notwithstanding its long pre-history, a reader has the unmistakable impression of a great spiritual figure in back of this sacred history, a character who gives unity to the narrative and around whom events revolve. That figure is Moses, the lawgiver of Sinai, who is not only the chief personality in Israel of the thirteenth century but the one who has exercised a constant and major influence on subsequent history.

"Since then no prophet has arisen in Israel like Moses, whom the Lord knew face to face. He had no equal in all the signs and wonders the Lord sent him to perform in the land of Egypt against Pharaoh and all his servants and against all his land, and for the might and the terrifying power that Moses exhibited in the sight of all Israel." (DEUT. 34:10-12)

As in the case of the entire Pentateuch, we are again amply justified in speaking of the substantial Mosaic authorship of *Deuteronomy*.

[*Suggested readings:*]

Chapters 1 to 4: Advance of the Israelites on the eastern side of the Jordan.

Chapters 9 to 11: Recapitulation of the Wilderness wanderings and exhortation to observe the Law.

Chapters 27 and 28: Summary of the Deuteronomic Code of Laws and the sanctions attached to the Law.

Chapters 32 to 34: The Song of Moses, exalting the beneficent power of God. This is followed by the Blessing of Moses, tribe by tribe, and a brief narration of the great Lawgiver's death on the plateau of Moab, in sight of the Promised Land.

JOSHUA:

On the eastern side of the Jordan, Moses and Joshua presented themselves before Yahweh at the Tent of Meeting, and Joshua received his divine commission to bring the Israelites into the Promised Land (*Numbers* 27:18-23). The account of how the successor of Moses fulfilled that mandate is contained in the *Book of Joshua*. The unknown author, making use of ancient documents, has taken up the thread of Israel's sacred history where *Deuteronomy* left off. He brings the narrative up to the moment when the tribes, now installed in their allotted territory, bury their great military hero in the hill country of Ephraim. As noted earlier, the Jewish Canon placed this work among the Prophetic Books, and not without reason. For they were aware that the author of *Joshua*, like many of the prophets, was portraying the unfolding of a divine plan which would be realized in spite of all obstacles. God's intervention in favor of His people was no accident.

"At your approach the Lord has driven out large and strong nations, and to this day no one has withstood you. One of you puts to flight a thousand, because it is the Lord, your God, Himself Who fights for you, as He promised you." (JOSHUA 23:9-10)

In the spirit of the prophets, the author saw beyond the apparently haphazard succession of victory and setback the divine purpose of establishing a holy nation in the Land of Promise. In *Joshua* this same Hebrew theology of history has found consistent expression. The Book is easily divided into two parts:

1. The passage of the Jordan and the successes by which the Hebrews captured a large part of the land of Canaan (1-12).

2. The allotment of the land and the final incidents in the life of the military leader (13-24).

As recent archaeological findings have emphasized, we are dealing with events which took place in the thirteenth century. The cities of Bethel, Lachish, and Tell Beit Mirsim (Debir) were destroyed by great conflagrations in that century, in all probability by the invading Israelites. It was not until the following century that the powerful Canaanite stronghold of Megiddo fell to the Israelites, whose slow, gradual conquest of the land is confirmed both by biblical tradition and modern archaeology. Jericho and Hai still remain problems for the archaeologist and the exegete, but a satisfactory solution may be expected in the not too distant future.

Somewhat to our disappointment the latest British-American excavations at Jericho (1952-1953), while reporting important new discoveries concerning the earliest periods of Jericho, have been able to tell us very little about the Late Bronze period (1500-1200 B.C.) of that ancient City. Because of the extensive denudation on the mound scant evidence remains to let us know what kind of a City it was during the Late Bronze Age and precisely when it fell to Joshua. Future campaigns at Jericho may yet disclose to us some of the secrets guarded by this famous old settlement, which was already two thousand years old when the forces of Joshua deployed before its walls.

The situation at Hai (which means "the Ruin"), a little more than ten miles to the west of Jericho, is even more perplexing. While the biblical account of its capture is fully described in the eighth chapter of *Joshua*, archaeologists claim that the City was destroyed around 2000 B.C. and not occupied again until 1200 B.C. How the biblical account is to be harmonized with the archaeological results thus far obtained remains a knotty problem, whose solution will probably be found only by future study and excavation.

Some of the noteworthy episodes in *Joshua* are the story of Rahab, the harlot, and the assistance she gave to the invading Hebrews (chap. 2), the taking of Jericho amidst the blast of the trumpets and the shout of the people (chap. 6), the stratagem by which Hai was reduced (chap. 8), and the victory of Joshua at Gibeon (chap. 10). This last episode is best known for the "sun" incident, preserved both in prose and in a fragment of very old Israelite poetry. Though we cannot determine precisely what took place on this occasion, the narrative has substantially preserved the record of a providential intervention of God in favor of His people. Once again, the writer gives a clear, theological interpretation of the event, in keeping with the spirit of the entire work which is describing God's gracious assistance to His people.

"The sun halted in the middle of the sky;
   not for a whole day did it resume its swift course.
Never before or since was there a day like this,
   when the Lord obeyed the voice of a man;
for the Lord fought for Israel." (JOSHUA 10:13-14)

The theme of *Joshua* finds typical expression in the hero's farewell speech to the people (chap. 23). In it he reminds them that it is Yahweh Himself Who has taken Israel's part and has delivered their enemies into their hands. To this the people, with one voice, answered: "Therefore we also will serve the Lord, for He is our God". The following *Book of Judges* is a sad record of their failure to live up to such promises. Not only because of his name ("Joshua" is the Hebrew form of the Holy

Name) but also because of his deeds, Joshua has become a type of Christ. His life and work are a dim foreshadowing of our own redemption.

[*Suggested readings:*]

Chapters 1 to 6: The crossing of the Jordan and capture of Jericho.

Chapter 10: The victory of Joshua at Gibeon.

Chapters 23 and 24: The final words of the aged chieftain, Joshua, and the solemn pledge of the people that they will remain faithful to Yahweh. Death of Joshua and his burial in the hill-country of Ephraim.

JUDGES:

The unknown author of *Judges* covers the history of Israel for a period of about two centuries, from the death of Joshua to the eve of Saul's kingship, in the middle of the eleventh century before Christ. The Book is a collection of epic-like stories of early national heroes who ruled Israel in periods of great danger, and often saved her from powerful and well-organized foes. The Book may be divided into three parts:

1. Introduction, describing conditions in Palestine just before the period of the Judges begins. (chapters 1 to 3:6)

2. History of the Judges. (chapters 3:7 to 16)

3. An Appendix, describing in some detail the migration of the tribe of Dan and the offense committed by the tribe of Benjamin. The latter incident gave rise to a bloody reprisal visited upon the offending tribe by the rest of the Israelites. (chapters 17 to 21)

The people of Israel now gave up their tents of the wilderness for permanent dwellings, gradually passing from the semi-nomadic to the sedentary form of life in the land of Canaan. This was a time of religious decadence and political disorder. The fight for the land was long and bitter, with no quarter asked or given. The twelve tribes felt the constant pressure of powerful and ruthless enemies, such as the native Canaanites, and the Philistines, newly arrived from their Aegean homeland. What was more serious, the purity of Yahwism, as revealed to Moses, was in great danger of being corrupted by the perverse religious practices of the Canaanites. Many of the Israelites, seduced by these lascivious rites, fell into idolatry and abandoned Yahweh. But God did not abandon them, even though He used the stern measure of humiliating subjection to bring them to their senses. The events narrated disclose a cycle which is often repeated in the history of Israel. This rhythmical historical pattern can be summarized in four terms: sin, punishment, repentance, deliverance. As often as they fell into idolatry, God's anger flared up against them; when they repented and cried to the Lord for help, He sent them a leader who rescued them. This is what is known as the divine pedagogy, or God's method of teaching His wayward people by the stern discipline of historical events.

The Song of Deborah (chap. 5) is a splendid example of that early Israelite poetry whose vigor reflects the primitive fervor of those ancient times.

"Hear, O kings! Give ear, O princes!
I will sing to the Lord my song,
    my hymn to the Lord, the God of Israel.

O Lord, when you went out from Seir,
    when you marched from the land of Edom,
The earth quaked and the heavens were shaken,
    while the clouds sent down showers.
Mountains trembled in the presence of the Lord,
    in the presence of the Lord, the God of Israel."
                                            (5:3-5)

Well-known also are the stories of Gideon, deliverer from the fierce Midianite invader (chapters 6 and 7), and of Jephte, the rash and ill-starred father who vowed the death of his own daughter (chap. 11). This very disconcerting episode is a reminder that the people of God were still men of their times, sharing many of the barbarous customs of their neighbors. Although not in any way endorsing these crude practices, the sacred writer has no intention of glossing them over or explaining them away. With the fine objectivity of every good historian, he records their faults as well as their virtues. In the Old Testament we are far from the moral perfection of the Sermon on the Mount. The story of the mighty judge, Samson, is an unforgettable piece of ancient literature. The hero was anything but an edifying character, but Yahweh was still able to accomplish His purposes even with so imperfect an instrument. The Samson narrative is of great value to the historian of the period because of its rich local color, depicting life in the Philistine Plain and the Shephelah. In general, the discerning reader will find more than a collection of good stories in *Judges;* underlying this vivid account of early life in Israel he will be able to make out the guiding hand of God, fashioning a sinful, stiff-necked people for a great destiny which was to be unfolded in the course of time. This development of history is beyond the power of man to control or to hinder permanently, for all history is ultimately in the hands of God. And when men have learned that the highest wisdom is to conform their wills to His, God will look with favor upon them. This is the enduring lesson of *Judges.*

[*Suggested readings:*]

Chapter 2: This serves as a preface to the history of the individual Judges, and gives a theological interpretation of both the reverses and successes which were to follow.

Chapters 6 to 8: The victory of Gideon over the camel-riding Midianites.

Chapters 13 to 16: The story of Samson.

RUTH:

The *Book of Ruth* is one of the masterpieces of world literature. In the form of a short story, the anonymous author tells us the history of a family which lived in the time of the Judges. Elimelech, a native of Bethlehem, went to Moab with his wife Naomi and their two sons, for famine had visited the land of Palestine. The sons married Moabite women, Orpha and Ruth. After the death of both Elimelech and the two sons, the bereaved Naomi set out for her homeland, bidding her daughters-in-law to remain in Moab. Orpha agreed but Ruth was determined to accompany Naomi and so she returned with her to Bethlehem. There she met Boaz, who married her in conformity with the *Levirate Law (Deut. 25:5-10)*. Ruth gave birth to a child who was called Obed, destined to be the grandfather of David. In this way an alien woman, Ruth of Moab, entered the genealogy of our Savior.

The story is told with consummate art. By delicate touches here and there we get an idyllic glimpse of the life of a pious family in ancient Israel. The characters display a courtesy, an unassuming piety which shows how deeply the religious spirit has permeated their everyday lives. The artist has succeeded in toning down the harshness of the rude and unsettled age of the Judges. Though many commentators date the composition in the Exile or after, there are strong arguments favoring a date as early as the seventh century. The Hebrew style, in its idiom and syntax, is equal to that of the best narrative portions of the *Books of Samuel*. To this may be added the following argument from the subject matter of the Book. A careful study of the customs reflected in the story, especially those concerning the marriage of Ruth and Boaz, has convinced many that the *Book of Ruth* has transmitted reminiscences of a state of customary law which preceded the general acceptance of Mosaic legislation.

The young Moabite widow, Ruth, has become an unforgettable model of filial piety, epitomized in those immortal words to Naomi: "Wherever you go I will go, wherever you lodge I will lodge, your people shall be my people, and your God my God." (1:16)

God's selection of Ruth for a place in the genealogy of His Son is a reminder that the Messianic blessings are not just for a chosen people but that all men are called to share them. The universality of God's will to save all men was never taught more gracefully.

FIRST AND SECOND BOOKS OF SAMUEL:

The two *Books of Samuel* originally formed a single unit. The Greek translation of the Old Testament, known as the *Septuagint, treated both Books as one historical work. Since they, together with the following two *Books of Kings*, described the fortunes of the Kingdom from its rise to its total disappearance in 587 B.C., the Septuagint translators grouped all four under one title, the "Books of the Kingdoms". St. Jerome, in his Latin translation of the Old Testament, modified the Septuagint title slightly and called them the "Four Books of Kings". They are found in our English Catholic bibles under that title. In retaining the title "Books of Samuel" we are following the ancient Hebrew tradition.

The *Books of Samuel* are largely the story of three men and the parts they played in the formation of the Hebrew monarchy. The three are Samuel, Saul, and David. The period of time covered by the narrative is a little over a hundred years, from the birth of Samuel to the last days of David. The title "Samuel" does not denote authorship, but, like the titles "Joshua", "Ruth", and "Esther", commemorates a key figure in the drama which is unfolded. As in the other historical books, it is clear that the author, or authors, made use of different sources, some of which are contemporaneous with the events described. An outstanding example of such an ancient and reliable source is the Court history of David, found in the second *Book of Samuel*, chapters 9 to 20. As a sample of accurate and vivid historical writing this section is unsurpassed in the ancient world. The final editing of the whole work probably took place in what is known as the Deuteronomic Period, around 600 B.C. In its final form the combined work shows the characteristic biblical concern not only for the historical facts but also for their theological interpretation.

Samuel, consecrated to the Lord from his youth, is the earliest of the prophets after Moses, and the last of the Judges in Israel. He delivered his people from the hands of the Philistines, traditional enemies of the Chosen People, and, in his days, the land was free from foreign oppression. At the command of God he anointed Saul as first king over Israel and finally, in Bethlehem, poured the sacred oil of consecration upon the head of David, in the midst of his brethren. "And the spirit of the Lord came upon David from that day forward." In the *Epistle to the Hebrews* 11:32, St. Paul pays tribute to Samuel as a man of faith.

Hardly a character in ancient history has been so strikingly portrayed as Saul, the son of Kish. This tragic figure, lofty in stature and strong in arm, but "troubled in spirit", dominates the first *Book of Samuel,* which describes his turbulent reign. The colorful and accurate portrayal of this complex and abnormal personality is unparalleled in ancient literary documents. The death of Saul and his three sons on Mt. Gilboa calls forth a touching lamentation from his successor, David.

> *"Thy beauty, O Israel!*
> *Upon thy high places is slain.*
> *How are the mighty fallen!* . . . (2 SAM. 1:19)

The way was now open for the brilliant career of Israel's greatest king. For seven years David ruled at Hebron over Judah alone; finally, at Jerusalem, he was proclaimed king over the twelve tribes, thus governing a united kingdom. It is in the second *Book of Samuel* that we are presented with a full-scale picture of this gifted and many-sided genius, who was likewise distinguished for his rare personal charm. As artist, general, and statesman, he stands out among the great leaders of Israel's past. His capture of Jerusalem, the City of the Jebusites, and his establishment of the capital on *Zion, have won for him a special place in Hebrew history. Not only as the king of a dynasty which is promised an eternal duration, but even as a man harassed by powerful enemies, David has become for the Christian a type of Christ. We recall that the phrase "Son of David" was one of the Messianic titles applied to Christ.

[*Suggested readings:*]

I Samuel:

Chapters 1 to 4: The miraculous birth of Samuel and his service with the priest Eli. The Canticle of Anna is one of the finest poems in the Old Testament.

Chapters 9 and 10: The manner in which Saul became king.

Chapters 16 and 17: The secret anointing of David and his triumph over Goliath.

Chapters 18 to 27: The friendship of David and Jonathan, and David's flight before the jealous Saul.

II Samuel:

Chapters 1 to 8: The death of Saul and the beginning of David's rule over united Israel and Judah.

Chapters 11 and 12: The sin of David. Rebuked by the Prophet Nathan he humbly acknowledges his guilt but is punished for his adultery.

Chapter 22: David's triumphant Hymn of Thanksgiving, which is duplicated, with slight variations, in *Psalm* 17.

Chapter 24: The Census of the united kingdom and David's purchase of the threshing floor which was later to be in the center of the Temple area.

FIRST AND SECOND BOOKS OF KINGS:

These two *Books of Kings* were originally a single historical work, and, as was said before, were once joined to the two *Books of Samuel* to form one large collection. The narrative in *Kings* brings the history of Israel from the death of David, around 961 B.C., to the brief notice of the kindly treatment given to Jehoiachin, prisoner of Babylon and last king of the royal house of Judah.

This last event takes us to a date shortly after the Fall of Jerusalem in 587 B.C. or, more precisely, to the accession of Evil-Merodach, King of Babylon, in 562 B.C. These four hundred critical years of Israelite history span the entire royal period with the exception of the reigns of Saul and David. The long account of the brilliant reign of Solomon serves as a majestic prologue to the work, describing the united kingdom in all its material splendor. The wisdom of Solomon, his great construction programs, the building of the Temple, and the extent of his wealth, have become proverbial. The unequalled height of prosperity attained in this era has been clearly attested by the twentieth century excavations of ancient Israelite sites. Megiddo, that proud old stronghold protecting the entrance to the Plain of Esdraelon, is one of those cities which has yielded up the secrets of its past. The spade of the archaeologist has now revealed at that site the well-constructed Stables of Solomon, once capable of holding at least 450 horses. On the Gulf of Aqabah, Professor Glueck has excavated Solomon's seaport, Ezion-Geber, the terminal of his far-flung commercial activities on the Red Sea and the Persian Gulf. At the same place a great copper smelter was also uncovered, belonging to the Solomonic Age, explaining one source of his fabulous wealth and illuminating the passage in *1 Kings* 7:46. Years ago it was fashionable to treat the Queen of Sheba incident as pure legend; now we know that it rests on solid historical grounds. Her famous visit to the court of Solomon has taken on new meaning, thanks to the expeditions of the American Foundation for the Study of Man in 1951 and 1952. This team of scholars studied the ancient city of Marib, once the great capital of the land of Sheba, and strategically placed on the great spice and incense trade routes of South Arabia. There can now be little doubt that the Queen came to the court of Solomon for the very business-like purpose of arranging a commercial agreement between the two countries.

Solomon's wealth and extensive building operations were achieved only at a great price, the crushing burden of taxation which drove his subjects to the point of rebellion. In his blindness and stupidity, Solomon's son Roboam stubbornly refused to alleviate their miseries and, in 922 B.C., the Kingdom was rent in two, never again to be united. Ten northern tribes followed the rebel leader, Jeroboam, two remained faithful to Roboam, and these latter constituted the tiny Kingdom of Judah which was to perpetuate the royal line of David. What follows after the Division (chap. 12) are parallel accounts of the two kingdoms, constructed according to the following stereotyped formulas:

a) Time when the king began to rule, synchronizing his rule with that of the other kingdom.

b) Duration of the rule of the king, whether in Judah or Israel.

c) A theological judgment passed on the reign as a whole. For the Northern Kingdom, this judgment is uniformly unfavorable.

d) Reference to the historical annals of either Judah or Israel, and a notice of the death and burial of the king. The Northern Kingdom of Israel, whose capital was Samaria, fell in 721 B.C. to Assyria, and then disappeared from history. Judah, the Southern Kingdom, survived this blow but met its fate with the destruction of Jerusalem in 587 B.C. by the Babylonians. This historical narrative is interrupted by the two lengthy cycles of Elijah and Elisha. The former was the great protagonist in Israel's life and death struggle against Canaanite *Baal worship, which threatened to contaminate and destroy the revealed religion of Yahweh.

At least three sources were at the disposal of the unknown author, whose intention and preoccupation must be learned from the use which he made of these sources. He was, of course, writing a religious history, the center of which was the Temple of Jerusalem where alone legitimate worship of Yahweh was offered. The influence of *Deuteronomy* on the final *redaction of *Kings* is evident. As far as the author was concerned, the essential clauses in the Covenant concluded between Yahweh and His chosen people were summed up in the phrase, "One God, one Temple". For those who had observed these clauses, like the pious King Josiah, there was unstinted praise in *Kings;* those who had neglected them were denounced and their evil end was interpreted as a judgment of God upon that negligence. This is history, to be sure, but it is that kind of history which the Germans call *Heilsgeschichte* (salvation history), where religious considerations are uppermost in the mind of the writer. The final edition of this work was issued probably during the Exile, when the ruined City and its once beautiful Temple could serve as a lasting memorial of Yahweh's just judgment on His wayward people. The throne of David had been overturned— but not for ever.

[*Suggested readings:*]

I Kings:

Chapters 3 to 11: The reign of Solomon.

Chapters 12 to 14: The great Schism in which the Kingdom is divided into North and South (Israel and Judah).

Chapters 17 to 22: The dramatic narrative of Elijah, champion of the religion of Yahweh.

II Kings:

Chapters 2 to 13: The history of Elisha, the extermination of the royal family in Israel, and the unjust usurpation and violent death of Queen Athaliah.

Chapter 19: The invasion of Sennacherib and his hasty lifting of the siege of Jerusalem.

Chapters 22 and 23: The reign of King Josiah who introduced a religious reform in the Kingdom of Judah.

Chapters 24 and 25: Destruction of Jerusalem and beginning of the Exile.

FIRST AND SECOND BOOKS OF CHRONICLES (PARALIPOMENON):

The two *Books of Chronicles,* called *Paralipomenon* in English Catholic bibles, once formed, with the books of *Ezra* and *Nehemiah,* one large historical work. The modern division into four distinct books, as in the case of *Samuel* and *Kings,* is due to the influence of the Septuagint. A comparison between the end of *II Chronicles* and the beginning of *Ezra* lends support to the tradition that these books formerly constituted a single, unified work. To this may be added arguments from style and general interest, the latter centering around the Temple and its cult, or liturgical functions. The identity of the Chronicler is unknown although some think it may have been Ezra himself. In any case, the author lived around 400 B.C., and not, as formerly supposed, in the early part of the third century. The writer must have had access to much ancient and precious historical material, over and above the sources used by the author of *Kings.* This material could have existed either in the form of long-standing oral traditions or literary documents which had been hitherto neglected. In contrast to the unjustified skepticism which once prevailed, scholars now recognize that the Chronicler has preserved for us some of the oldest and most reliable traditions of the Kingdom of Judah.

A glance at the historical situation of the Jews at this time will help to explain the purpose of the author in drawing up this history. Now that Israel's political glory was a thing of the past, he wished to show that the true vocation of the chosen people was to offer God the homage of an undefiled cult in the Temple of Jerusalem, still the center of their national life. The events of the sixth century must be understood if we would grasp the intention of the Chronicler. The Decree of Cyrus the Great in 538 B.C. permitted the exiled Jews to return from the Babylonian Captivity which had lasted about fifty years. But such a permission did not involve a grant of complete national autonomy and the restoration of the Davidic kingship. Palestine still remained under the rule, however benign, of the kings of Persia. Not national and worldly glory, but religious zeal would have to be, from now on, the source of Jewish strength and greatness. The Chronicler's chief purpose was to assist in this important transformation from a politically independent society to a religious community without political aspirations. In this post-Exilic community we are able to discern some of the basic traits of that Judaism which affords the religious backdrop to the New Testament. When the Chronicler introduces a long review of Jewish history, which is the substance of his work, the purpose is to show that Israel's hope does not lie in her military strength or her political wisdom, but in fidelity to the Covenant. When the Lord appeared to Solomon by night He repeated that message which was first heard by David from the lips of Nathan:

"And as for you, if you walk before Me as David your father walked, and do according to all that I have commanded you, and keep My statutes and My ordinances; then I will establish the throne of your kingdom, as I promised to David your father, saying: There shall not fail a man of your seed to be ruler in Israel." (II CHRON. 7:17-18)

Yahweh, the God of history, in Whose hands are the destinies of men and nations, did not need their armies nor their shrewd alliances. But He wanted their obedience.

The Chronicler belonged to that all too rare class of historians who are able to discern, beyond the interplay of seemingly isolated events, the workings of God in history. The annalists of Assyria and Babylon have left us the shattered fragments of their own boastful records; but they did not write creative, meaningful history. Israel, tiny and provincial though she was, has handed down to us a theology of history, grounded in her own faith and hope. She who alone came to know, in her moments of crisis, that her fate and that of the whole world was ultimately under the one divine Providence was the first to write history in the fullest and best sense of the word. The two Books may be divided as follows:

I Chronicles: Judah's prehistory, from Adam to Saul, made up largely of genealogies (chaps. 1 to 9). Death of Saul and the reign of David (chaps. 10 to 29).

II Chronicles: The reign of Solomon (chaps. 1 to 9). The history of Judah from the division of the Kingdom (922) to the Edict of Cyrus (chaps. 10 to 36).

Three passages of singular power and beauty should be noted:

a)   The two prayers of David (*I Chron.* 17 and 29).
b)   Solomon's prayer for wisdom (*II Chron.* 1).
c)   The Dedication of the Temple (*II Chron.* 6 and 7).

*   *   *   *   *   *

CHRONOLOGY OF THE PERSIAN PERIOD:

Edict of Cyrus — 538 B.C.
Cambyses — 530 to 522
Darius I (the Great) — 522 to 486
Second Temple finished and dedicated — 515
Xerxes I — 486 to 465
Artaxerxes I (Longimanus) — 465 to 424
Overthrow of the Persian Empire by Alexander the Great — 333

EZRA AND NEHEMIAH:

These two Books cover the period of Israel's history from the Return under Zerubbabel to the last days of Nehemiah, the zealous rebuilder of the walls of Jerusalem. The historical value of the *Books of Ezra and Nehemiah* is enhanced by the fact that they are practically the only sources we have for the history of Israel in the Persian Period, which lasted a little over two centuries. A vexing historical problem confronts the student of the era of Restoration. It is the chronological order of the two leading figures of the Period, Ezra and Nehemiah. Who was the first to come from the Babylonian community to the city of Jerusalem? The traditional view is that Ezra came to Jerusalem in the seventh year of Artaxerxes I (458 B.C.), while Nehemiah, the cupbearer of Artaxerxes I, received permission to return in the twentieth year of the same ruler (445). A long and impressive list of scholars has challenged the traditional view, maintaining that Nehemiah arrived and began his work before the coming of Ezra. New evidence may settle the question which must, for the moment, remain open.

Among the sources which the authors used are the Memoirs of Ezra, Aramaic letters from the Persian archives, the Autobiography of Nehemiah, and various registers of returning exiles such as we find in the second chapter of *Ezra*. The autobiographical portions of *Nehemiah* (chaps. 1 to 7, and parts of 12 and 13) give us a most vivid and authentic picture of the man, and help us to pierce the darkness which envelops Jewish history in the fifth century before Christ.

Both Books are compilatory in character, their style and language show marked variations, the narrative is often uneven, and little attention has been paid to strict chronological arrangement. In general, Ezra's leadership was most evident in spiritual matters. He was interested in religious and cultic reform and contributed much to the formation of what is now know as Judaism. Beginning with the Restoration of the exiles in the Persian Period, the name "Judaism" is generally given to the religion of that period and what came after it, thus distinguishing it from the religion of the preceding centuries which is called the "religion of Israel". The foundations of Judaism are associated, by both Jewish tradition and modern criticism, with the name of Ezra. With him began the attempt to fix a normative theology and a basic legal system for the entire Jewish community. This development of Juda-

ism's characteristic institutions, especially school and synagogue, reached its definitive stage in the second century of
the Christian Era.

Nehemiah assumed the task of restoring the great City
Wall of Jerusalem, since he was deeply moved by the re-
port that the Holy City lay open on all sides to the attacks
of hostile neighbors. In memory of his single-minded
devotion to the Jewish cause Ben Sira concluded his "Praise
of the Fathers of Old" (*Ecclesiasticus* 44:1 to 49:13) with
mention of Nehemiah, "who raised up our ruins and
healed our breaches". By this time (around 400 B.C.) the
restored community was well established, due in no small
measure to the zeal of men like Ezra, Nehemiah, the
prophets Haggai and Zechariah, and others, not to forget
the generous autonomy granted the Jews by the Persian
Empire. From this time, the priesthood became more
influential, religious life centered more and more about the
great Temple Area, and the Law took the place of the
prophets, who had left no successors in Israel. The Judaism we know partially from the Gospels was in process of
formation, and it was a way of life stamped with a strongly legalistic character.

It would be a serious mistake, however, to think that
the Judaism of this period was so rigid and exclusive as to
be shut off from all foreign influences, including Greek
influence. Nothing could be farther from the truth, as
literary and archaeological evidence has amply demonstra-
ted. Along with these numerous contacts the Jew of
Palestine never completely lost sight of that part of the
community which made up the Diaspora, with its chief
centers in Babylon and Alexandria. So it came about that
Judaism, though it took root in the soil of Palestine under

the leadership of men like Ezra and Nehemiah, extended
its influence far beyond the tiny district of Judah which
was still a *satrapy of the Persian Empire. This influence
reached the densely populated centers of the ancient world,
all united under the sway of Persia until the arrival of
Alexander in 333 B.C. With the victorious coming of the
great Macedonian general we are in a new historical era,
to be known as the *Hellenistic Period.

[*Suggested readings:*]

Ezra:

   Chapter 1: The Edict of Cyrus and the beginning of the Return
from Exile.

   Chapters 3 to 6: Rebuilding of the Temple and opposition of the
Samaritans.

   Chapter 9: The prayer of Ezra.

Nehemiah:

   Chapters 1 to 6: The rebuilding of the walls of Jerusalem in spite
of Samaritan opposition. This is narrated in the first person.

   Chapters 8 to 10: The public reading of the Law and the renewal
of the Covenant.

BOOK OF TOBIAS:

   This and the following Book belong among the Deuterocanonical Writings, which are not accepted in the Jewish
and Protestant Canons of sacred writings, but are included
in the Catholic Canon of Sacred Scripture. The Catholic
Canon was quite universally professed in the earliest ages
of the Church and was solemnly defined at the Council of
Trent (1546) and reaffirmed at the Vatican Council
(1870). Apart from occasional doubts expressed by some
of the early Fathers of the Church, there has been no hesitation among Catholics in acknowledging their legitimate

place in the list of sacred writings. Non-Catholics call our Deuterocanonical Books the "Apocrypha". The terminology should be noted in order to avoid confusion, because Catholics call "Apocrypha" books which have no place in their Canon.

This charming short story, *Tobias*, introduces the reader to a pious Israelite family living at Nineveh during the exile of the northern tribes of Israel. It will be recalled that they were led into captivity after the Fall of Samaria in 721 B.C. The unknown author wrote long after the events portrayed in the story, probably as late as the third century B.C. This opinion gains support from the fact that his work faithfully reflects Jewish standards of piety at a time when a century of contact with Hellenism called for a restatement of Jewish religious ideals.

Tobit, the father of the hero, is represented as a Jew of Galilee zealous for the observance of the Law. Deported to Nineveh by the Assyrians he continued his works of piety but misfortune overtook him in the form of blindness. In his great distress Tobit prayed that he might die (3:1-6). In the meantime, a kinswoman of Tobit, Sarah of Ecbatana in Media, offered the same prayer because of the strange misfortune which had overtaken her. Seven suitors of Sarah had met death in the bridal chamber. A link between the two desperate people was forged in the person of the young man, Tobias, who was sent by his father to recover a sum of money in Media. With the assistance of the Archangel Raphael, Tobias overcame all dangers, recovered the sum, married Sarah, and put the evil demon to flight. Upon the return of Tobias and Sarah to Nineveh, Tobit regained his sight with the gall of the fish caught by Tobias. Raphael, after exhorting the family to prayer, fasting and almsgiving, vanished from their sight. The aged Tobit, grateful for the favors God had bestowed on him and his family, sang a beautiful hymn of praise in which he foretold the restoration of Jerusalem (chap. 13). Tobit lived to a ripe old age and Tobias, acceding to his father's dying wish that he take refuge in Media, lived to rejoice in the violent overthrow of wicked Nineveh.

The key to understanding this work, and several others like it in the Old Testament, is a knowledge of its literary type or form. It is important, therefore, to determine, as far as we can, the category of literature to which *Tobias* belongs. The more common view is that it should be classed as edifying religious literature and that the fictional element predominates over the historical. That there is an historical nucleus in the story is quite certain but we are simply unable to draw any clear line between what is historical and what is edifying fiction. To classify the work as didactic fiction is not in any way meant to minimize its value. Our Lord Himself has shown how fictional narratives can be used to teach the most important religious truths. *Tobias* is a didactic story whose lessons certainly were not lost on Jewish readers. Not only does it inculcate such virtues as care for the dead and almsgiving, along with deep filial piety, but it also teaches the nearness of God to troubled man and the benevolent Providence He exercises over His children. Those who are tempted to interpret this delightful story in too rigid and literal a fashion might ponder the words of one commentator: "This Book was not written to give us a cure for physical blindness, but for our spiritual blindness."

BOOK OF JUDITH:

The plot of this stirring narrative opens with an account of the reprisals ordered by Nebuchadnezzar against his Palestinian vassals. The Assyrian general, Holofernes, accepted the royal commission to punish the rebellious Jews, and after devastating the surrounding countries, appeared at the gates of Bethulia. This was a little town close to the Plain of Esdraelon. The besieged city was about to surrender when the pious widow, Judith, bravely took up the cause of her disheartened people. Arrayed in her finest garments, she gained access to the tent of Holofernes, and while he was in a drunken stupor, slew the savage enemy of Israel. The Assyrians, upon hearing the news, fled in all directions, and nothing remained for the Hebrews but to gather up the booty left by the panic-stricken foe. The Book closes with a beautiful hymn of triumph (chap. 15), praising Judith and thanking God Who had once again intervened to save His people.

Is *Judith* history, fiction, or a combination of both? The student of the ancient world, although recognizing many familiar names and places, will see at once that historical and geographical incongruities abound in this short Book. Persons and places are found in very curious juxtaposition. From these very inconsistencies we perhaps obtain our clue to the intention of the author. It seems that he did not intend to write a history in the strict sense and that he expected his readers to have the good sense to recognize that. Making Nebuchadnezzar the King of Assyria is one warning on that score. He was actually the King of Babylon who destroyed Jerusalem in 587 B.C. Again, the author seems to have mingled together actual events from different epochs. At the same time one cannot fail to see there are solid historical elements in the story. Perhaps the writer intended to choose as characters for his narrative those men and people who were long established as the enemies of the Jews. Lumping them together in one narrative might prove to be disconcerting, but it made thrilling reading and the point of the story could not be missed. Nebuchadnezzar was certainly a fitting symbol of the Jewish enemy, just as Assyria was a symbol of cruel oppression to Israel and the rest of the Near East.

Historical facts, therefore, make up the substance of the vivid narrative but the dimension of time is lost or completely disregarded; accurate chronology does not interest the author. Because we have no parallel type of literature in our own language we cannot conclude that this kind of composition would make no sense to a Jew of the pre-Christian era. The solution here proposed is neither new nor better than probable. It has been proposed and ably defended by Father Lefebvre in his article on *Judith* for the Supplement to the *Dictionnaire de la Bible.* The difficult and unfamiliar literary form, which we find in *Judith,* demands more study before we can fully appreciate the intention of the sacred writer.

In *Judith* the author has, in any case, succeeded in telling a fascinating story. But his purpose did not stop there because he had an important lesson to teach his readers. They needed to be instructed as well as entertained. From the stirring events which took place around Bethulia, the reader was to learn that God is the master of history and that He triumphs over all adversaries. What God asks of His followers is faith, and for a Jew of this period that meant a faith which issues in the observance of the Law and in a humble, prayerful acknowledgement of our dependence on Him. These are some of the lessons of the *Book of Judith,* whose composition is now dated by most scholars between the second and the first centuries before Christ.

ESTHER:

The *Book of Esther* has come down to us in two forms, represented by a Hebrew and a Greek text. The Church, in solemnly pronouncing on the canonicity of the sacred writings at the Council of Trent, defined the canonicity of *Esther,* including the parts written in Greek. These Greek sections, which St. Jerome placed in an appendix to his translation of the Hebrew text, are called the Deuterocanonical parts of *Esther.* The chief witnesses to the Greek text are the three great Christian *codices, the *Sinaiticus, the *Vaticanus, and the *Alexandrinus. St. Jerome knew of an Aramaic text of the Book which he used in making his Latin translation.

The story relates how Esther, a Jewish maiden in the Persian capital of Susa, rose to the dignity of Queen to Ahasuerus, the Jewish name for Xerxes. Soon after, a Persian courtier, Haman by name, became first minister in the Persian Empire and the king ordered all to bow down before him. One man resolutely refused, the Benjaminite Mordecai, loving foster-father of Esther. Enraged by this supposed affront to his dignity, Haman determined to exterminate the Jews resident in Persia, and then confiscate all their goods. Confident that the king would readily accede to his cruel demands, Haman prepared a special gallows for his personal enemy, Mordecai. But Esther, instructed by her foster-father, successfully interceded with the king and turned the tables on the plotting vizier who was hanged on the gallows he had prepared for Mordecai. After Mordecai had been elevated to the position left vacant by Haman, he issued an edict allowing the Jews to defend themselves against their assailants. On the 13th day of the month *Adar the Jews slew 75,000 of their enemies. Two days later the victory was solemnly celebrated and the Jews were ordered to commemorate annually this great event, henceforth known as the Feast of *Purim.

All Catholic scholars admit that there is at least a nucleus of historical fact in *Esther,* without being able, however, to draw a satisfactory distinction between the historical and the fictional. It seems undeniable that the author has used his creative imagination to heighten the interest of this absorbing story. The liberty which the Greek translators have taken with the Hebrew original is probably a hint that they saw in *Esther,* not so much a strict historical document, as a work of edification, and treated it as such. Nevertheless, the more we learn about life in the Persian Empire under the *Achaemenian kings the greater becomes our respect for *Esther* as a reliable picture of that historical period. Besides the strongly accented spirit of nationalism which pervades the story the author also has a religious purpose in view. What he wishes to impress on his co-religionists is God's loving care over them, and then the need of approaching God with humility and confidence in His assistance. Mordecai's message to Esther, now seated upon the throne as Queen, sums up with terse eloquence the doctrine of the Book:

"Think not that you will save your life in the royal palace, any more than the rest of the Jews. For if you remain silent at this time, relief and deliverance shall come

to the Jews from another quarter, but you and your father's house will perish; and who knows whether you have not come to royal estate for such a time as this?" (4:13-14)

FIRST AND SECOND MACCABEES:

Unlike the Books of *Samuel* and *Kings* these two Books do not, in any sense, form a unified, continuous narrative. Rather they are parallel accounts of the same general period, that of the Maccabean Revolt, but they differ greatly in their style, contents, and manner of treatment. The union of the two Books is, accordingly, quite artificial and arbitrary. It can be justified, however, inasmuch as both deal with the same hero, Judas Maccabeus, and both are concerned with the liberation of the Jewish nation from the *Seleucid yoke. Each work is listed among the Deuterocanonical writings and each has come down to us in a Greek text.

First Maccabees, a composition of very high literary and historical value, was written a little more than a hundred years before Christ, by an enthusiastic supporter of the *Hasmonean House. The author, who seems to have been a resident of Jerusalem, wrote in Hebrew or Aramaic, but this text has perished and only the Greek version survives. After an introductory chapter explaining the division of the Empire of Alexander among his generals, the narrative describes the turbulent days from the reign of Antiochus IV Epiphanes (175 to 163 B.C.) to the death of Simon, head of the newly-constituted Jewish State (135 B.C.). Within this short space of forty years, the Jews had successfully resisted the tyranny of Antiochus IV, who sought to impose the Hellenistic way of life on all Palestine. Through the brilliant leadership of Judas and his successors, the Jews managed, for a short time, to gain complete political independence. It was of brief duration, to be sure, and their hard won independence was lost completely with the coming, in 63 B.C., of the Roman general Pompey, who took control of Jerusalem and all Palestine in the name of Rome.

The author of *First Maccabees* was not only an excellent historian but perhaps even an eye-witness of some of the events he narrated. The deeper significance of this life-and-death struggle against overwhelming odds did not escape this keen observer. He understood the power of a religious cause to stir men up to heroic deeds and astounding acts of self-sacrifice. Besides his own personal involvement in events, he seems to have had many opportunities to acquire accurate information about the struggle and the complex political situation of that day. For the tiny country was beset not only with enemies from without but with traitors from within. Participation in the campaigns gave him a detailed knowledge of the geography and topography of Palestine. His religious fervor was transparent, showing itself in a great love of the Law and anything connected with the Temple. This is especially evident in his moving account of how Judas Maccabeus purified the defiled Temple and dedicated the new altar of sacrifice, in the year 164 B.C. Every year, usually in the month of December, the Jewish people celebrate this Feast, which is known as *Hanukkah, or the Feast of Dedication.

In *Second Maccabees* the unknown author informs us (2:23) that he has abridged a five volume history of the period, written by a certain Jason of Cyrene. Beyond the general aim of instructing and edifying his Greek-speaking

countrymen, the author's interest in the observance of
the Sabbath and other practices, together with his explicit
teaching of the resurrection of the body (7:11 and 14:46),
stamps this Book as one of the earliest examples of the
Pharisaic viewpoint. We know from the New Testament
(*Matt.* 22:23 and *Acts* 23:6-8) that the resurrection of
the body was a major point of controversy between *Sadducees and *Pharisees. Since the Pharisees play an important part in the unfolding of the New Testament
drama, it is of some interest to see their teaching coloring
a piece of literature in the pre-Christian era.

While both Books deal with the same subject, the
Maccabean Revolt, the difference in point of view, emphasis, and language is very marked. *Second Maccabees*
opens just before the accession of Antiochus Epiphanes,
and terminates with the death of the Seleucid general,
Nicanor. This latter event takes place shortly before the
death of the great national hero, Judas Maccabeus. The
author himself clearly states his intention:

*"Accordingly, I beg those who read this book not to
be dejected by such misfortunes but to consider that these
punishments were meant, not for the destruction of our
people, but for their correction. For it is a sign of great
benevolence not to let the sinful alone for a long time
but to punish them swiftly. For with other nations the
Lord waits patiently so that when the day of judgment
comes he may punish them according to the full measure
of their sins; but with us he has acted differently, so that
he does not take vengeance on us when our sins have
reached their height. Therefore he never withdraws his
mercy from us, and even though he disciplines us with
misfortune, he does not forsake his own people."* (II MAC.
6:12-16)

The Book covers a period of but fifteen years, a span which is covered by the first seven chapters of *First Maccabees*. Written probably in Alexandria towards the end of the second century B.C., it served to strengthen the morale and religious fervor of the Jews who lived in that great Hellenistic center of the Diaspora.

The task of preacher seems more congenial to the writer than that of sober historian. With warmth and energy he exhorts his readers to see the hand of God in those events which enkindled the patriotism of the Jews and finally brought religious freedom to the chosen people.

With the exception of the *Book of Wisdom*, no other writing of the Old Testament teaches so clearly the immortality of the soul, and even the resurrection of the body. This teaching of eternal happiness with God after a virtuous life on earth was meant to be the solace of every pious Jew when he had to undergo persecution for his faith. The memorable picture of the aged martyr, Eleazar, who "welcomed a glorious death in preference to a life of sinful idolatry", the martyr-mother and her seven sons, the many fervent exhortations to prayer, especially for the dead, the reminders of the intercessory power of the saints, all these have accounted for the great popularity of the Book in the Christian era.

[*Suggested readings:*]

First Maccabees:

    Chapters 1 and 2: The causes of the Maccabean Revolt.
    Chapter 3: Judas Maccabeus and the beginnings of the Revolt.
    Chapter 8: The alliance with Rome.
    Chapter 14: The reign of Simon and his achievements.

Second Maccabees:

Chapter 2: The author describes his work of summarizing the five-volume history written by Jason of Cyrene.

Chapter 3: The attempted sacrilege of Heliodorus and its frustration by divine intervention.

Chapters 5 to 7: Persecution of Antiochus Epiphanes and the martyrdom of Eleazar and the seven brothers.

Chapters 8 to 10: The early successes of Judas Maccabeus, death of Antiochus, and the Purification of the Temple.

THE PROPHETS

ISAIAH:

Isaiah, the greatest of the Prophets, was born in Jerusalem around 765 B.C. His family probably belonged to the aristocracy of the Kingdom of Judah but we have no reason for believing that he belonged to the royal line. The imagery of this great religious poet bears the stamp of his origins. It is taken from scenes in Jerusalem and the vineyards round about. He speaks of the Waters of Shiloh, the Upper Pool of the City. He is thoroughly familiar with the Temple area and he is present at the hour of sacrifice. He satirically describes the mincing steps of the fashionable and haughty daughters of Zion who grind down the poor. For understanding the message of Isaiah and, as far as we can, the interior life of the man, no chapter in the Book is more important than the sixth. Here the call to the prophetic office is described. It was the year that King Uzziah died (740 B.C.), bringing to an end a period of great material prosperity for the tiny Kingdom. Isaiah had gone up to the Temple to assist at the sacrifice, and there he was granted a vision of God in all His holiness and majesty. The summons was given and Isaiah, his lips now purified, uttered his brief sentence of acceptance, "Here am I; send me!" The influence of that overwhelming experience is discernible in all of his subsequent work.

Isaiah became the adviser of Ahaz, whose Kingdom was threatened by the North Israel-Damascus coalition drawn up against him. But the weak and hesitant king turned a deaf ear to the message of Isaiah (chap. 7), which contains the famous "Emmanuel" prophecy. The Virgin-birth of a Child is offered to Ahaz as a sign that Judah has nothing to fear from the two powers which threaten him. But Ahaz had lost faith and, in desperation, he called upon Assyria for help. Judah was momentarily saved, but only at the price of bearing the heavy yoke of Assyria.

Hezekiah, the successor of Ahaz, tried to break this yoke and allowed himself, against the stern warnings of Isaiah, to be dominated by the anti-Assyrian faction in Jerusalem. Assyria acted quickly and Sennacherib's army was soon at the gates of Jerusalem. In Sennacherib's famous Inscription he tells us that Hezekiah was "shut up like a bird in his cage". Though the City was mysteriously and providentially relieved (*Is.* 37:9-36), the Kingdom was now devastated, as we see from Isaiah's vivid picture in chapter 1:5-9. Isaiah never lost faith in Yahweh and, despite the ruin all about, he still knew that God would save a remnant. He made this belief more real by naming his son "Shear Yashub" (a remnant shall return). We know very little about the last days of this great spiritual leader whom God raised up at a critical period of Israel's history. An ancient tradition says that he was sawed in two under the impious king Manasses, thus climaxing his life's work with martyrdom. The prophecy is divided into two very distinct parts:

I.   (chaps. 1 to 39) These chapters faithfully reflect, by and large, the life and thought of the eighth century in the Kingdom of Judah. They contain speeches and poems, spoken or written on different occasions, and assembled here without much attention being paid to chronological sequence. This "anthological" character of the work is found in many of the prophetic collections. It is extremely important that we recognize this fact and not expect to find uninterrupted temporal and thought sequence in the prophetic writings. The "Book of Emmanuel" (chaps. 6 to 12), occasioned by Judah's War with the Israel-Damascus axis, is very important for its Messianic teaching. Many of these passages, which point ahead to Christ, have been incorporated in the Liturgy of the Church.

Isaiah is a prophet both of judgment and salvation, judgment because the people have deserted Yahweh and sought after false gods; and salvation, because Yahweh, despite their infidelities, will never forget His covenant. Both judgment and salvation are beautifully portrayed in chapters 24 to 27, a section which is commonly called the "Apocalypse of Isaiah". He shows himself here, as elsewhere, preeminently the prophet of faith.

Not only in *Isaiah,* but in many other prophetic collections, we find numerous threats directed against the pagan nations among whom Israel was to work out her destiny. When the people forgot Yahweh and lapsed into sin, especially the sin of idolatry, God punished them, often using these nations as the instruments of His wrath. Recall the words of Isaiah:

> *"Oh! Assyria, the rod of my anger,*
> *And the staff of my fury!*
> *Against a godless nation will I send him,*
> *And against the people of my wrath will I charge him,*
> *To despoil them, and to seize them as prey,*
> *And to trample them down like mud of the streets."*
>
> (10:5-6)

God, as the Master of history, uses historical events as a means to teach men. History is the sphere of His judgments. For this reason, Assyria, Babylon, Egypt, Canaan, Aram, and a host of others, appear frequently in the inspired writings as the instruments of God's chastisement. But their own time is not far off! For their own sins God reserves a terrible punishment which is often announced by the prophets. These dreadful calamities are the "burdens" of the nations of the ancient East. They who devoured others will, in turn, be swallowed up by stronger nations, for Yahweh's control is universal and no nation can escape the punishment of its iniquity. This is the prophetic interpretation of history, founded upon the justice of God and the inevitability of judgment.

II.   (chaps. 40 to 66) This part of the prophecy is known as Deutero-Isaiah (Second Isaiah), because scholars generally attribute the authorship of this part to a writer who lived in the period of the Exile. The Decree of the Biblical Commission in 1908 on the unity of authorship in *Isaiah* reflects an older tradition among Catholics. However, the Commission's carefully worded decision, that the evidence at hand in 1908 against the unity of authorship did not compel assent, was not meant to remove the question from all further research and debate. Even though the matter is not yet settled to the satisfaction of all, an increasing number of Catholic scholars either hold the author to be a later and unknown disciple of the "Isaiah School", or at least they recognize that the historical and theological background is that of the Exile and, for the later chapters, the Restoration. The first fifteen chapters of this part are called the "Book of Consolation", opening with the words, "Comfort ye, comfort ye, My people". Within this series of consoling promises to Judah in her Exile, are interspersed the Servant Songs, depicting the Suffering Servant of Yahweh. For the first and only time in the Old Testament we see suffering depicted as expiatory and as the way to glorification. Christ, in His Passion and Glorification, was to be the perfect realization of the Suffering Servant. Chapter 53 is the climax of these Songs. Because of its striking resemblance to the Gospel narrative of Christ's suffering and death, Isaiah has been called the "Evangelist of the Passion".

[*Suggested readings:*]

Chapters 1 to 5: The "Great Arraignment" of Judah and the imminent judgment.

Chapter 6: The call of Isaiah.

Chapters 7 to 9: The Emmanuel prophecies.

Chapter 11: The reign of peace under a ruler of David's line.

Chapter 19: The "burden" of Egypt.

Chapters 34 and 35: The contrasted future of Edom and Israel.

Chapters 42 to 53: The Servant Songs.

JEREMIAH:

The substance of Jeremiah's prophetic vocation was essentially the same as that of any other prophet—to preach the word of Yahweh to a wayward people which persisted in following false gods. But, unlike many prophets, Jeremiah has revealed much of his interior life, and the inner struggle which this sensitive man faced in accepting the responsibilities of his vocation. He was born around 650 B.C. in the tiny village of Anatoth, a distance of about an hour and a half's walk from Jerusalem. Though naturally of a timid and introspective disposition, Yahweh had great plans for this remarkable man:

> *"Behold, I have put My words in your mouth;*
> *See, I have set you this day over the nations*
> *   and over the kingdoms,*
> *To root out, and to pull down,*

> *To destroy and to overthrow,*
> *To build and to plant."* (1:10)

Reminded by God that he was chosen for this work even before his birth, Jeremiah could only stammer out his own unworthiness:

"And I said: 'Ah, ah, ah, Lord God; behold, I cannot speak, for I am a child'." (1:6)

It is interesting to compare the reactions of Isaiah and Jeremiah to the call of Yahweh. Though every natural impulse of his sensitive nature rebelled against the task, Jeremiah manfully acceded to the divine summons and set about his ungrateful task. The prophecy itself reveals how, through the grace of God, the stuttering lad of Anatoth became a "fortified city, an iron pillar and a wall of brass against the kings of Judah". (1:18)

His career can be divided into three phases:

I.   627 to 609 B.C. Jeremiah threw himself wholeheartedly in back of the Reform of Josiah, inaugurated by the finding, in 621, of that code of laws which some identify with *Deuteronomy*. But the men of Judah were not to be reformed overnight, and they soon relapsed into their old idolatry and oppression of the poor. A crisis was reached in 609 with the death of the pious King Josiah, and the second period of Jeremiah's ministry began.

II.   609 to 597 B.C. These were his most difficult years, as he watched the impending doom approach from the north. Both king and priest opposed Jeremiah, and even his loyalty to his country was questioned. The period ended with the first deportation of his countrymen to Babylon.

III. 597 to 587 B.C. As the counsellor of Zedekiah, a weak man who was set on the throne by the victorious Babylonians, Jeremiah had constantly to fight against the false prophets. Looking only to personal gain, these men aroused in the people dangerous and illusory hopes of deliverance. In vain did Jeremiah warn them that resistance to the overwhelming power of Babylon was futile. Foolishly relying on the "broken reed", Egypt, Zedekiah dared to rebel against Babylon. Vengeance was swift and terrible; Jerusalem was levelled to the ground in 587, and the people were led across the Desert into exile.

In 1935 and 1938 the brilliant archaeologist, James Starkey, discovered a collection of about twenty ostraca (broken pottery with writing on one side) in the ruins of the Judean city of Lachish. The ostraca turned out to be letters, written in the excellent classical Hebrew of that period with which we are familiar through the prose sections of Jeremiah. The letters were addressed to the commander of the garrison of Lachish which was a powerful fortress serving as one of the western outposts guarding the city of Jerusalem. This extraordinary discovery of documents contemporaneous with Jeremiah, has given us a brief but life-like picture of the situation which prevailed in Judah shortly before the fall of its Capital.

Jeremiah remained amidst the ruins of his beloved Jerusalem but was later kidnapped by rebellious Jews and forced to accompany them into Egypt where he died. We have no precise information on his last days. Though he knew frustration and defeat in his lifetime, the posthumous influence of Jeremiah has been very great. One scholar has said of him: "Without this extraordinary man the religious history of humanity would have followed a different course". The need for a renewal of spirit and an interiorizing of religion was one of the great lessons of his prophecy. This became a dominant theme in later writings, especially in *Ezekiel*. As a man, Jeremiah was a tragic figure of the innocent sufferer. In this way he became a fitting type of Christ, the Man of Sorrows, Who offers His life for His people.

[*Suggested readings:*]

Chapter 1: The call of Jeremiah.

Chapters 2 to 6: The sin of Judah, the faithless lover.

Chapters 18 and 19: Lessons to be learned from the potter and his clay vessel.

Chapters 21 to 23: The judgment of Jeremiah on kings and prophets of Judah.

Chapters 30 to 33: The promises of Restoration.

Chapters 50 to 52: The prophecy against Babylon, and a description of the capture of Jerusalem in 587 B.C.

LAMENTATIONS:

These are five elegies which commemorate the destruction of the Holy City by Nebuchadnezzar in 587 B.C. Their importance in the Catholic Liturgy of Holy Week is well known; no writings are more suitable for setting the tone of this holy season. The author does not wish, primarily, to describe the great national catastrophe which weighed so heavily on Jewish hearts. There was no need to relive every scene of the last act. But he seeks to arouse our compassion and pity and to draw for us the lessons of this awful event. The most poignant details are selected by the eye-witness author in order to achieve and to heighten the effect he intends to produce. There is conscious art in this work, and no aspect of the common grief is neglected. The student should note the artificial literary arrangement of four of these dirges. They are alphabetic acrostics in which the verses, or stanzas, begin severally with the successive twenty-two letters of the Hebrew alphabet. Yet, the artificiality of the scheme in no way diminishes the pathos of these religious poems.

The five songs of lament also give us an insight into the loftiest spiritual attitude of Israel in the face of its great tragedy. Though her days were filled with anguish, Israel's hope in the permanence of God's plan for His chosen people was as unshakeable as ever. Even though Mt. Zion was destroyed, Yahweh's pledge of fidelity to the Virgin of Zion remained, and He would bring back His people. The consciousness of national guilt is very acute in these poems. The people of Judah had defied Yahweh and gone after false gods; their punishment was just and deserved. Note that the familiar figure of Israel as the bride of Yahweh is sustained; but now Jerusalem is a desolate widow. Both Christian and Jewish tradition attribute the *Lamentations* to the great prophet, Jeremiah, who was a witness of Jerusalem's destruction. Many parallels in ideas, sentiments, and vocabulary, between the prophecy of Jeremiah and the *Lamentations* support this tradition. But the arguments in favor of the Jeremian authorship of the work are not conclusive, and it may be the work of another writer who came under the influence of Jeremiah, an eye-witness of the national catastrophe.

BARUCH:

The *Book of Baruch* is traditionally attributed to the secretary of Jeremiah. Some scholars, for various reasons, ascribe the work to one or more unknown authors of the post-exilic period. If the latter opinion is true, we would have but another instance of that familiar literary device of attaching a work to some well-known character of Israelite history. The Book has come down to us only in Greek, though much of it may have been written originally in Hebrew. If one insists on crediting the work to the historical Baruch, he should also hold that it was written in a Semitic language, whether Hebrew or Aramaic.

The first part, extending to chap. 3:8 is a moving summons to Israel, the sinful nation, calling her to national penance. Joined to this is a fervent prayer to God, asking for mercy and forgiveness. The second part contains a beautiful hymn to wisdom and an exhortation to strive after it. The Book closes in a spirit of great joy and hope, for, like the prophets of an earlier age, the author assures his readers that God will never forget His people. Jerusalem, in its renewed splendor, will be repeopled when its children return from their captivity. Attached to *Baruch* is the *Letter of Jeremiah,* meant to appear as a message sent by the Prophet to the captives in Babylon. This Letter, whose author is unknown, was probably ascribed to the Prophet because of its superficial resemblance to the letter which Jeremiah actually sent to the exiles of 597 B.C. (*Jer.* 29:1-23). The present Letter appears to paraphrase the tenth chapter of *Jeremiah* where we read a similar denunciation of idolatry. The religious leaders of Israel were obliged at all times to maintain constant vigilance lest idolatry and its licentious practices should take root in Israel and corrupt the purity of Yahwism. Contact with foreign people inevitably brought with it this danger, whether from Canaanite or Greek. Consequently, much of the Old Testament and many of its most ardent passages are powerful protests against the inroads of idolatry which always threatened the vigor and uniqueness of their divinely revealed monotheism.

EZEKIEL:

Ezekiel is the leading spiritual figure of Judaism during the Exile. Furthermore, he is the first spokesman of God to exercise the prophetic office outside of the Holy Land. What Jeremiah did for his countrymen in Jerusalem, Ezekiel did for the exiles in Babylon, denouncing their sins when necessary and restoring their hopes when all seemed lost. Before the complete destruction of Jerusalem in 587, Ezekiel, like his great contemporary, had to fight against an unusual state of mind which had taken hold of the people. Blindly trusting in their own privilege as a chosen group, and in the presumed inviolability of the Holy City, they sought a sudden, divine intervention which would restore them to a new and greater Jerusalem. False prophets had nourished these delusions by their lying promises. To these blinded compatriots, "a rebellious house", Ezekiel was obliged to announce that the fall of Jerusalem was inevitable—and that it would come quickly.

"*And My hand shall come upon the prophets who see illusions and foretell lies. They shall not belong to the community of My people, nor shall they be recorded in the register of the house of Israel, nor shall they enter the land of Israel. Thus you shall know that I am the Lord God. Because, yea, because they led My people astray, saying 'Peace!' although there was no peace. The people are like a man building a wall, and they daub it with whitewash.*" (13:9-10)

The first deportation of Jews took place in 597. Ezekiel

was a member of this group, which was settled by the Babylonian authorities at Tel-Abib by the River Chebar. The location is now to be identified with the Kabar Canal near *Nippur, a waterway mentioned in cuneiform documents of the Persian period. Five years later Ezekiel received his call, fully but mysteriously described in the first three chapters. From this time until 587 he assumed the responsibility of preparing the "rebellious house" for the total destruction of Jerusalem and its Temple, interpreting for them the theological meaning of this severe punishment.

Symbolic actions and visions play a large part in this prophecy. The eating of the scroll, the siege of Jerusalem sketched on the sun-baked tile, the immobility of the prophet, and the cutting off of his hair, are some of these better known symbols. They have always appealed to the oriental imagination and serve a useful didactic purpose. The impending doom is often portrayed by means of this imagery but the prophecy is not restricted to threats. Ezekiel is somewhat of an innovator insofar as he rises above the traditional doctrine of collective responsibility, to set a new emphasis on the individual as the object of divine justice. No longer shall they hear the old proverb, "The fathers have eaten sour grapes, and the children's teeth are set on edge". Henceforth, if a man acts justly in his lifetime he shall be saved; if he sins, that man shall die. Though Ezekiel does not give us anything like a fully developed doctrine of immortality, as we find it in the *Book of Wisdom*, he has prepared the way for this revelation by insisting on the responsibility of the individual.

The exiles were disheartened and disillusioned by news of the fall of Jerusalem. To these Ezekiel was to bring the comforting revelation that, despite the momentary victory of the enemy, God would triumph in the end, when He had brought about a restoration of the scattered faithful to Zion. The most powerful expression of this message is found in chapter 37, where Ezekiel, standing in the midst of a great valley, saw the dry bones brought to life by the vivifying breath of God. So, too, would the house of Israel come to life and return to the land where Yahweh would renew His eternal covenant with her. Besides this Messianic doctrine with its perspectives reaching far into the future, Ezekiel laid the groundwork for the restored community and its cultic life. The last eight chapters, based on a vision granted him by God, describe in detail the dimensions of the ideal Temple and the ritual ordinances to be observed in restored Judaism. However unattractive this last part of the Book may be to the modern reader, it has had a far-reaching influence on the restored Jewish community. Little wonder, then, that Ezekiel has been called the "Father of Judaism". Though rarely cited in the New Testament, there are many points of contact between the imagery of the *Apocalypse* of St. John and the visions of Ezekiel. Christian art is heavily indebted to the Prophet for some of its favorite symbols, such as the "four creatures" of the first chapter who have been taken as emblems of the four Evangelists.

[*Suggested readings:*]

Chapters 2 and 3: The vocation of Ezekiel.

Chapters 5 to 7: The punishment of Judah.

Chapters 26 to 28: The prophecies against Tyre.

Chapters 33 and 34: The function of a prophet and the replacement of evil shepherds by the Shepherd of David's line.

Chapter 37: The vision in the valley of dry bones. At the word of the Prophet they are restored to life.

DANIEL:

The *Book of Daniel* takes its name from the central character in the work rather than from any alleged authorship. In the Hebrew Canon of Scripture the Book is ranged among the "Writings", but in the Greek version, *Daniel* is found among the Prophets, and some additions have been made which are of a Deuterocanonical nature. The Book can be divided into two parts, with an appendix of three short stories.

I. (chapters 1 to 6) Episodes in the life of Daniel, a Jewish youth brought into Exile at the time Jerusalem fell. The stories relate a series of triumphs over adversity. A Jew of the early second century B.C., victim of the persecution of Antiochus Epiphanes, would quickly see the application of these stories to his own circumstances.

II. (chapters 7 to 12) These contain visions of an apocalyptic character, narrated in the first person. Apocalyptic writing comes at a late date in the Old Testament and grows out of the principles which the prophets proclaimed. In a style which is often mysterious and obscure the authors of apocalyptic writings proclaim the inevitability of judgment and the ultimate triumph of God over His adversaries. While these writings, with their strange symbols and obscure visions, must not be interpreted with the same literalness with which we interpret a prosaic historical narrative, we should not overlook the permanent and often profound theological truths veiled under this unfamiliar and difficult style. With their unshakeable trust in the triumph of God and their certitude of His control over history, they have left us a very early specimen of a literary form which culminates in the *Apocalypse* of St. John.

Daniel differs sharply from the prophetic writings in its almost exclusive preoccupation with the future, whereas all the other prophets are concerned, first of all, with the present. Instead of the usual prophetic threats and castigations, it is the vision of a distant and obscure future which prevails in *Daniel*. Here we are dealing neither with conventional historical narrative nor simple biography, but with a special category of literature. It would, of course, be going much too far to assert that *Daniel* rests on no historical foundations. The more we learn about the late-Babylonian period the greater is our respect for the historical elements incorporated in the Book. The lessons of *Daniel* are important for any age but especially for one in which the Church suffers some great trial. From the very first chapter, Daniel and his companions are represented as offering heroic resistance to pagans who would lead them into idolatry. They become types of those martyrs who prefer death to apostasy.

In the highly imaginative visions of the last six chapters the great powers of the ancient world rise up to contend with God, only to give place to a Kingdom which shall have no end. Scholars have long debated the question as to whether the author had in mind a specific historical situation. The most probable view is that the writer was thinking of the persecution of Antiochus Epiphanes (168 B.C.), and that the Book, as it now stands, comes from this period, and that it was meant to comfort the Jews in their ordeal.

The verses referring to the Son of Man in *Daniel* 7:13-14 still puzzle the commentator. Both Jewish and Christian tradition maintain that the passage is Messianic, though there is little agreement among scholars when it comes to detailed interpretation. The phrase "Son of Man" is taken up in the New Testament by our Lord Who frequently applies the title to Himself. It was most suitable to express, not only His eternal pre-existence in heaven, but also His everlasting dominion which He, as Messiah, has received from the Father.

The episodes of Susanna, Bel, and the Dragon, all written in Greek, are edifying short stories which have been added to the original work.

HOSEA:

In the Hebrew Bible the *Book of Hosea* heads the collection known as the "Twelve Minor Prophets". Hosea, whose name, "Yahweh saves", is etymologically identical with the Holy Name, was a native of the Northern Kingdom and began his prophetic career in the last years of Jeroboam II (786-746). His activity continued during the brief but chaotic period immediately following the death of Jeroboam, and ceased in the reign of Menahem (745-738). There is no reason to believe that he witnessed the fall of Samaria in 721. Personal tragedy, which had saddened his life, exerted a great influence on his message. From his unfortunate marriage with Gomer, who proved to be a faithless spouse, Hosea learned a lesson of enduring value. Gomer is a figure of Israel, the beloved of Yahweh. God is the jealous Lover Who chastises His beloved, not to annihilate, but to bring her back to the fresh and pure joy of their first love.

The infidelity of Israel, which began even before she inherited the Promised Land, was expressed in her idolatrous worship, her disobedience to the Law of God, her lying, cheating, and oppression of the poor. The soul of

Israel was sick and no amount of sacrifices, mechanically offered, could restore her to health and the true service of Yahweh. Only punishment would bring her to her senses; by despoiling her of her rich ornaments which her false lovers had given her, Israel would, in her misery, recall the days of her youth when she was faithful to her true Lover. Once again, a humiliated Israel would seek Yahweh.

Though the question is still argued, the marriage with Gomer is, in all probability, a real event in the life of the prophet, and neither a vision nor an allegory. The eleventh chapter of *Hosea* is one of the most magnificent passages of biblical literature, proclaiming the ineffable love of Yahweh for His people. It is an unequalled poetic expression of the divine compassion. Hosea is the first to express the relation between Yahweh and Israel in terms of marriage, a symbol which has become classic in Old Testament literature. In the New Testament, both St. John and St. Paul express, in terms of conjugal love, the union between Christ and His Church. (See *II Cor.* 11:2, *Ephesians* 5: 25-33; *Apocal.* 19:7 ; 21:1-5)

JOEL:

Of the prophet Joel we know nothing except the name of his father. We are entirely dependent on the contents of the Prophecy in the matter of determining its date. In this case, the evidence is not altogether clear and yields no certain conclusion. The work, which contains very powerful and highly imaginative poetry, can be divided into two parts:

I. (chapters 1 and 2) These concern a present calamity in which a great plague of locusts is devastating the land. The prophet exhorts the people to lamentation, fasting, and supplication, in order that Yahweh may cause it to cease. In the last part of this section, an abrupt intervention of Yahweh brings about the restoration of peace and prosperity. The people now know that Yahweh is "in the midst of Israel".

II.   (chapters 3 and 4) This part differs from the first in that it is apocalyptic, looking to the future and the approaching Day of Yahweh. On that dreadful Day only he who calls upon the Name of the Lord will be delivered. This is also the Day on which Yahweh will judge the enemies of Israel and destroy them. Jerusalem shall never again suffer invasion from the hordes of Assyria or Babylon, for the Lord shall dwell in Zion and protect His Holy City. Though we cannot determine the date of this collection with certainty, the probabilities favor the period after the Exile, better known as the Persian era.

AMOS:

Amos was a contemporary of Hosea and exercised his prophetic ministry during the prosperous reign of Jeroboam II. Though a native of the Southern Kingdom he preached his message in the North, chiefly at the great shrine of Bethel. Amos was a shepherd of Tekoa, a tiny village to the southeast of Bethlehem. In the summer he descended from his rugged hills to the maritime plain known as the Shephelah, and there served as a dresser of sycamore trees. The poetry of Amos is filled with imagery taken from his own background. More important still, the simplicity of his pastoral life made him singularly sensitive to the luxury and callousness of the wealthy people of the North.

His prophecy opens with a sweeping indictment of

Damascus, the Philistines, Tyre, Edom, and other countries bordering on Palestine. Yahweh is no mere national god; His sovereignty extends over all people. Yet Israel had no right to be complacent. The Day of Yahweh was coming and it was to be a Day on which God would punish an Israel blinded by temporary prosperity and deaf to God's demand for justice. Amos not only preached a clear-cut monotheism to this nation which was so prone to idolatry; he spoke of a God Who, unlike the gods of the surrounding countries, hated the disorder of sin, injustice, and cruelty to the weak, no matter where it originated. The sin of Israel had become so great that pardon no longer seemed possible; chastisement was inevitable. Of what use to multiply their feasts and their sacrifices, thinking that thereby the divine wrath would be appeased? God took no pleasure in their solemn assemblies or mere external rites unaccompanied by a change of heart. "Let judgment well up as waters, and justice as a mighty stream" is the divine command.

Like the other prophets of Israel to whom God had spoken, Amos knew that the threatened punishment was but a means to a future goal, hidden in the merciful counsels of Yahweh. God's love for man is beyond all human reckoning, and even the perversity of the human will is not able to frustrate the designs of God. For this reason the prophecy closes on a note of hope, which lights up the darkness of impending doom.

"And I will turn the captivity of My people Israel,
And they shall build the waste cities and inhabit them."
(9:14)

Under the image of material prosperity, Amos points ahead to the Messianic era, when the Savior will redeem all men from the captivity of sin. Because he constantly hammers at the injustice of the rich, Amos has been called the "Prophet of Social Justice".

OBADIAH:

This is the shortest Book in the Old Testament. Aside from the name, we know nothing of the author whose message is one of woe for Edom, a traditional enemy of Israel. Though earlier material may be incorporated, the prophecy itself belongs to the period following the destruction of Jerusalem in 587. Southern Juda had been devastated by the army of Nebuchadnezzar, and the Edomites, perhaps with the approval of Babylon, moved into southern Judah. They came from their traditional home in the savage and mountainous country below Moab. By the time of the Persian period they were well established in the southern hill-country of Judah and, before Nehemiah rebuilt the City Wall, were able to attack the Holy City almost at will. The prophecy of disaster in this Book closely resembles the prophecy against Edom in the 49th chapter of *Jeremiah*.

JONAH:

The Book is named for the central figure in the story, not because it was written by Jonah. Instead of treating the work as history in the severely modern sense of the word, Catholics are now more inclined to interpret it as a parable. The lesson it teaches is a most important one, the all-embracing character of God's love. The author repudiates the narrow and exclusive belief of some Jews that God's holy purposes are limited to the people of Israel. In passing, it can be said that one of the minor lessons taught is the uselessness of attempting to escape a duty imposed by God.

Written by an unknown author, probably in the fifth century B.C., the protagonist of the drama, Jonah, represents an outlook or mentality which was all too prevalent in that period. Aware of being the object of God's special election, many of the Jews developed a narrow nationalism which restricted the future Messianic blessings to Israel. The author of *Jonah,* not without a sense of humor, protested against this religious snobbishness. Nineveh, the wicked City of the pagans, and ancient persecutor of Israel, was doomed to destruction and Jonah was sent to announce it. But the City repented and God stayed His avenging arm, much to the chagrin of the prophet who had momentarily forgotten that the mercy of God is limitless. This parable could be characterized as a satire against a kind of provincialism which sought to limit God's love of man. Such writing has helped to prepare the way for the Gospel and its message of redemption for all, Jew or Gentile.

MICAH:

Like most of the prophetic books, the prophecy of *Micah* is a collection of pronouncements uttered at different times and places, and probably arranged in their present form by a later editor. The prophecy may be divided into three parts:

I. (chapters 1 to 3) The coming judgment of Yahweh. The tone is one of rebuke and denunciation.

II. (chapters 4 and 5) The glory of the restored Zion. It will become the spiritual center of the world.

III.   (chapters 6 to 7) The case against Israel, argued by the Prophet, who represents Yahweh, the plaintiff. This sombre picture closes with a beautiful expression of confidence in God's mercy.

The anthological character of the composition is evident from the way in which threats and promises, condemnation and encouragement, alternate. Micah, whose name means "Who is like Yahweh?", was a contemporary of Isaiah. He came from Moreseth, a little village in the southwest of Judah. As a member of the poorer class, he wrote with a deep sympathy for the common man, victimized by wealthy proprietors and false leaders. While Isaiah tells us more about the political events of this time, Micah confined his preaching almost exclusively to religious and ethical questions. In the New Testament the mystery of the Nativity is the fulfillment of Micah's prophecy that the Davidic Messiah should come from Bethlehem. (5:1)

NAHUM:

This prophecy must be dated in the years preceding the fall of the great Capital of Assyria, Nineveh, in the year 612. Nahum's cry of triumph at the awful destruction is but a prediction of the joy which ran through all the ancient world when the word went abroad, "Nineveh is laid waste!" A coalition of Babylonians and Medes succeeded in reducing the proud City, after many years of fighting. The assault of the foe, the carnage in the streets, the moaning of the vanquished, and finally, the awful silence of the deserted City, are described with unparalleled vividness in the second chapter. The third chapter speaks bitterly of the "bloody city". It is clear that this epithet is no exaggeration when we read the royal inscriptions of the Assyrian kings who boasted of their ruthlessness in war and unbridled cruelty to the vanquished. But the composition is not a work of pure and unrestrained revenge, even if it is less directly spiritual than the prophecies of *Hosea, Micah* and others. We find in *Nahum* an authentic religious protest against the brutalities of the ancient foe, a poetic vindication of Yahweh's authority over all nations, and an expression of hope for peace and justice, two characteristics of the Messianic future. The downfall of Nineveh was a judgment of God on the wicked City. Jerusalem was to learn, before many years passed, the meaning of such a judgment.

ZEPHANIAH:

The opening verses of the prophecy set the ministry of Zephaniah, which means "Yahweh has treasured", in the reign of the pious King Josiah (640-609 B.C.). Indications in the work itself, such as the protests against pro-Assyrian factions, the cult of Baal and Mesopotamian divinities, and the condemnation of the court ministers rather than the king, help us to place the work in the earlier part of Josiah's reign, perhaps in the decade 640 to 630. We can distinguish three parts:

I. (chapter 1) The threat which is directed against Judah and Jerusalem. The Day of Yahweh is at hand, pictured as a great sacrifice in which Judah will be offered as the victim. The medieval hymn *Dies Irae*, which is the Sequence in the Requiem Mass of the Catholic Liturgy, borrows heavily from this chapter.

II. (chapters 2 to 3:7) This contains an admonition to Judah, calling upon her to repent. If Judah refuses she will be engulfed in a great catastrophe which will overwhelm friend and foe alike.

III.   (chapters 3:8-20) This section is a promise to the remnant of Israel which will survive the purifying trial. Though there is no proof of direct borrowing, it is very probable that Jeremiah, who came shortly after Zephaniah, had been influenced by him in both language and ideas.

HABAKKUK:

Habakkuk was a contemporary of Jeremiah and wrote his prophecy between 605 and 589 B.C., that is, between the great Babylonian victory at *Carchemish and the beginning of the Babylonian invasion of Judah. The first two chapters are cast in the form of a dialogue between the prophet and Yahweh. Habakkuk announces the coming of the Babylonians as the instruments of Yahweh's chastisement. At the same time, the poet seeks to justify the unsearchable ways of God in allowing the new world power, Babylon, to be the chastising rod in His hand.

The third chapter serves as a magnificent religious lyric, whose literary form and meaning have been brilliantly illuminated by the recovery of the ancient Canaanite literature of *Ras Shamra, in northern Syria. The widespread use of such a distinctive poetic device as repetitive *parallelism, puts this psalm, from a literary viewpoint, in the tradition of ancient Canaanite poetry. In this ode Yahweh appears in all His splendor and executes vengeance on Judah's enemies. It ends on a note of joyful confidence in Yahweh, Whose dominion extends over the whole world.

HAGGAI:

In the second year of Darius, 520 B.C., Haggai and Zechariah came forward to urge on the rebuilding of the Temple. The prophecy of Haggai dates from this period, more precisely the summer months of 520. The third, rather than the first person, has been chosen, probably to give greater solemnity to his message. At the center of his interest was the Temple of Jerusalem. Its reconstruction seemed to Haggai to be a necessary prelude to the coming of the Messianic era when the nations would come hurrying to Zion. This interest, added to his close association with the priests, has led some scholars to believe that Haggai was a prophet attached to the sanctuary in Jerusalem. The style of the prophecy is simple and straightforward, in keeping with the practical end he had in view.

ZECHARIAH:

Zechariah was a contemporary of Haggai and his co-worker in promoting the rebuilding of the Temple, and the resumption of its cultic functions. His prophecy is made up of two very distinct parts:

I. (chapters 1 to 8) After a brief but fervent call to repentance, the prophet describes, in obscure and symbolic language, a series of eight visions. All of these are calculated to encourage Zerubbabel and the High Priest, Joshua, in their work of reconstruction. An angel interprets each vision for the prophet. Chapter eight brings this section to a close with a description of Zion in the Messianic era, when many nations shall come to seek Yahweh in the Holy City.

II.   (chapters 9 to 14) There is, at present, agreement neither on the period in which this part was composed, nor on its authorship. Opinions vary from the eighth to the third century B.C. Despite the present uncertainty and the general unwillingness of scholars to assign it to the prophet himself, new historical and archaeological evidence may change the picture and oblige us to assign the work to Zechariah in the last quarter of the sixth century. Chapter nine pictures the Messianic King as just and humble, riding on the lowly beast of burden. Our Lord fulfilled this prophecy on the first Palm Sunday (*Matt.* 21:4)

MALACHI:

This prophecy is the work of an author who wrote in the Persian period, shortly before Nehemiah's arrival in Jerusalem. Apart from what we can gather from the work itself, we know little or nothing about the author who is the last of the writing prophets. His name, Malachi, is probably a shortened form of "Mal'akiyah", which means "My messenger is Yahweh". By his trenchant criticism of the abuses and religious indifference which had already begun to sap the strength of the restored community, the author was preparing the way for the reform measures of Ezra and Nehemiah. In line with the great prophets, he reminds the Jews of Yahweh's love for them, and their sorry return of that love. Yahweh is wearied with their laxity, and, above all, with the tepidity of their priests. For all who have shown themselves unfaithful, the Day of Yahweh is coming. Israel can avoid this judgment only by a widespread and thorough reform of her cultic service, together with a strict observance of the Mosaic Law. In the first chapter, while denouncing the carelessness of the priests who have offered blemished sacrifices, the author looks ahead to another day when a pure oblation shall be offered to God by all the nations. The perspective of this prophecy is Messianic, and its fulfillment is found in the Holy Sacrifice of the Mass.

"For from the rising of the sun even to its setting, my name is great among the Gentiles, and in every place there is sacrifice, and there is offered to my name a clean oblation: for my name is great among the Gentiles, says the Lord of hosts." (1:11)

THE SAPIENTIAL BOOKS

The search for the "good life", and the grappling with such profound problems as suffering and retribution, are not innovations of the Old Testament. Nor is that quest formulated in a type of literature peculiar to the Jewish people. The Old Testament itself is well aware of the international character of Wisdom literature. We read, for example, in *I Kings* 5:12 that "Solomon's wisdom excelled the wisdom of all the children of the East Country and all the wisdom of Egypt". Long before the inspired scribes set pen to papyrus, wise men in Egypt as well as Mesopotamia were posing those questions which have always fascinated and sometimes vexed the spirit of man. What becomes of man when he dies? Wherein lies true success in this life? How is it that innocent men suffer and the wicked seem to prosper? These are the questions men asked themselves in the Valley of the Nile as well as on the sun-baked plains of Mesopotamia. Voluminous wisdom materials from Egypt are now extant, for in Egypt the exceedingly dry climate and the hot sands have wonderfully preserved the papyri on which their speculations are recorded. Soil and climate have not been as generous in Mesopotamia, but we know now that such speculations go back to the earliest times in that region. Thus, for the first time, it is now possible to see Hebrew Wisdom literature against its ancient oriental background. To give but one illustration, Egyptian Wisdom literature is often ascribed either to a king or to a minister high in the affairs of state, thus giving a certain prestige to the writing. This practice may help us to understand the long tradition in Israel which makes Solomon the author or the central figure in its Wisdom literature, although we know that most of our literature of this type is anonymous.

The new knowledge of oriental wisdom, which is increasing every day, not only gives us a broader perspective, but shows how far the inspired sage surpassed his pagan forerunner, who had only his own human lights to guide him. Hebrew sapiential writing embodies not only the wisdom of man, but, above all, the wisdom of God, teaching us lessons which are valid for all ages. In God's own way this literature has prepared the way for the Gospel, which alone can fully answer the anxious problems raised by these wise men of Israel. For "behold, a greater than Solomon is here" (*Luke* 11:31).

JOB:

The Prologue of this religious masterpiece introduces a sturdy, patriarchal character, who, though not an Israelite, was renowned for his piety and uprightness. Satan, or the Adversary, obtained God's permission to test the genuineness of his virtue, and a series of misfortunes befell the hero from the Land of Uz (Edom). Brought to the brink of despair by his utter misery, the tragic sufferer cursed the day of his birth and longed for death as a release from his pain. But he never denied God even in the most extreme anguish.

Having heard of his misfortune, the friends of Job gathered around the wretched man and a long dialogue ensued, in which the three men, vain comforters, sought to convince Job that his suffering was due to sin. Against this point of view, which represented a traditional and commonly held belief in Israel, Job solemnly protested his innocence and appealed to God as his Vindicator. With the intervention of God the debate was closed, but not without Job having humbly bowed before the inscrutable

designs of a just and all-knowing God. The story is
rounded off with a prose Epilogue which informs us that
the trial is ended.

The properly dramatic parts of *Job* are confined to the
Prologue and the Epilogue; the long dialogue which inter-
venes is sublime religious poetry but it cannot be classified
as drama. It is now generally recognized that the author
was using traditional materials, that is, a well-known theme
as the setting for the problem he wished to discuss. We
meet a "Job" in *Ezekiel* 14:14, 20, and the name occurs
in such widely separated literature as Egyptian Execration
texts of the twentieth century B.C., the Mari Letters of
the eighteenth century from Mesopotamia, and the
Amarna Letters of the fourteenth century from the land
of Canaan. Some kind of historical nucleus, resting on
age-old traditions, is therefore very likely, even though
the "historical" element is relatively unimportant.

The substance of the Book is didactic, and is found in
the long poetic dialogue between Job and his friends; to
these we may add the speeches of Yahweh and the enig-
matic Elihu, who appears quite suddenly on the scene
(chap. 32). There are numerous obscurities of language
and thought, and some textual corruptions, though the
text has undoubtedly suffered more at the hands of textual
critics than it has through the process of transmission.
The dialogue contains some of the most sublime poetry
in the Old Testament. Yahweh's first speech to Job, in
chapters 38 and 39, surpasses all other descriptions of the
Creator and His work whether in the Bible itself or in
any other literature. The apt illustrations and sublime
imagery combine to form a poem of singular strength
and brilliance. The author obviously stands in wonder

and adoration before the infinite power and wisdom of God.

As already noted, many of the themes in sapiential writing were common to the literature of the ancient world. The subject matter of *Job,* for example, is closely related to a Babylonian work which is far older than our composition. But the Hebrew poem, in which we see a man's soul refined and tempered in affliction, is far more profound in its spiritual lessons, and much superior even from a literary point of view.

The task our author set himself was no easy one. He wished to reconcile the justice and wisdom of God with the facts of experience in its most bitter form—the suffering of an innocent man. It would be a mistake to look for a complete solution of this problem in this Book alone, or, for that matter, in any other book of the Old Testament. Nor does the solution offered bring us to the sublime New Testament portrait of Him Who alone can give meaning to innocent suffering. Job was not a Christian and it would be wrong to seek a Christian answer to the problem at this stage of Old Testament revelation. The Hebrew theory of retribution, with some exceptions, held that man suffered only because of his sins; misfortune was simply the punishment for sin. Job knew that this did not hold in his own case. Conscious of his own innocence before God, he had to find a solution to his suffering elsewhere. The key to his heroism and the reason for his vindication by God is Job's unshaken conviction of the divine justice. Despite the obscurity of his own vision, and the severe testing of his faith by suffering, this man of anguish never for a moment doubted the justice of God. And his final words were a moving appeal, in all humility and faith, to the divine tribunal (chap. 31).

The great merit of Job, the innocent sufferer, is to have rendered testimony to the unity of the God of justice and the God Who allows man to suffer. That the two are identical is certain, but the problem of reconciling them remained a problem for the human mind. That mystery found magnificent expression in the poem on Wisdom in chapter 28:

> *"But where can Wisdom be found?*
> *And where is the place of understanding?*
> *Man knows not the way of it,*
> *Nor is it found in the land of the living."* (28:12, 13)

Suffering is a great mystery, hidden in the innermost counsels of God. To accept the enigma of suffering demands a humility and greatness of soul which recognizes its inability to say the last word on all things, and especially on its own troubled existence. This is the great lesson of *Job* and it provides a salutary and necessary preamble for the later revelation which will come in the New Testament. The solution will then be centered in Christ, the innocent and voluntary Sufferer, Who has given meaning to our lives as well as to our sufferings.

[*Suggested readings:*]

Chapters 1 to 3: The prologue, setting the stage for the debate. This is followed by Job's first speech.

Chapters 9, 10, and 19: Job speaks in the bitterness of his soul. But he still has confidence that God will vindicate him.

Chapter 29: The former happiness of Job.

Chapters 38 and 39: Yahweh's first speech, demanding humble submission to His designs.

Chapter 42: The submission of Job and the restoration to his former prosperity.

THE PSALMS:

The word "psalm" is from the Greek, and denotes a poem recited or sung to the accompaniment of a musical instrument. In the Hebrew Bible the title of the collection is *Sepher Tehillim* or "Book of Praises", emphasizing one of the common traits of these poems addressed to Yahweh. The canonical Psalter contains 150 of these sacred songs, which made up the official prayer and hymn book of the ancient Hebrews. No other book in the Old Testament gives us a more comprehensive or authoritative expression of Israel's religion, from the earliest times to the Hellenistic period. Though secular poetry undoubtedly existed in Israel, as we know from a few drinking and harvest songs which have been preserved, only its religious lyrics have come down to us in any quantity.

Like the five Books of the Law, and perhaps in imitation of their arrangement, the *Psalms* are divided into five Books, separated by liturgical conclusions which are called "doxologies" (several verses of exultant praise). These liturgical conclusions give us a hint that the collections were formed originally for use in public worship. The five Books are arranged in the following manner:

Psalms 1 to 41. The "Yahwist" Collection, attributed in practically its entirety to David. In this group the name of Yahweh occurs more than 270 times.

Psalms 42 to 72. The "Elohist" Collection, so called because the divine name "Elohim" is used so frequently (164 times). The variation in the divine name is best explained by assuming that, at the time of the compilation, one name enjoyed a current preference over the other.

Psalms 73 to 89. The Psalms of Asaph, one of David's three chief musicians, are a feature of this collection.

Psalms 90 to 106. This Book includes the psalms celebrating Yahweh's kingship which is to come at the end of time. His kingdom will be one of sanctity and justice. These psalms prepare the way for the Kingship of Christ, which is established with the coming of the Son of God.

Psalms 107 to 150. This is a miscellaneous group of songs, including several "alphabetic" psalms, each of whose twenty-two verses begins with a letter of the Hebrew alphabet. A similar artificial arrangement is found in the *Lamentations* of Jeremiah, as we have seen.

Many of the Psalms were used in the Temple liturgy both before and after the Exile, but not a few of them have a very individual, non-cultic character which expresses the personal religious experience of a man. It is an exaggeration, accordingly, to try and connect all the Psalms with public cult. Frequently the author of the psalm is unknown but there is no solid reason for denying that many of them come from David himself whose skill on the lyre as well as in poetic composition is well attested in Hebrew tradition. There are also good grounds for believing that David played a major part in the organization of Israelite religious music.

Though many details still elude us, we are today in a much better position to appreciate the structure of Hebrew poetry, and even the elusive question of Hebrew metrics. This is largely due to the sensational discovery of the Canaanite literature from *Ugarit, once a thriving port at the eastern end of the Mediterranean. It should be noted that "Canaanite" is the older name for the Phoenicians. The value of this recent discovery for biblical studies can hardly be exaggerated, for we are now in a position to see how much the Israelites, especially their poets, borrowed from their Canaanite predecessors. This dependence is considerable in such matters as structure, imagery, and vocabulary. Such a characteristic trait of Hebrew poetry as parallelism, or the symmetric balancing of clauses, is now seen to go back to ancient models. It should be obvious, of course, that this dependence on earlier models does not in the least diminish the essential superiority of the *Psalms* over their morally crude forerunners. As elsewhere in the Old Testament, similarities in style and vocabulary must not blind us to the profound differences between the *Psalms* and Canaanite poetry. In spiritual and moral significance the *Psalms,* and the Old Testament in general, are unmatched in the literature of the ancient Near East.

Much work has been done recently in attempting to classify the *Psalms* according to general headings or groups. It will help our understanding of this rich and varied poetry to note some of the larger categories or types into which the *Psalms* easily fall:

1. *Hymns.* Psalms 8, 18, 28, 95 to 98.
2. *Prayers.* Psalms 3, 11, 19, 43.
3. *Didactic Psalms.* Psalms 1, 13, 14, 77, 89.
4. *Prophetic Psalms.* Psalms 2, 21, 71, 109. These are the chief Messianic Psalms which point ahead to the coming of Christ.

N.B. The Psalms listed above follow the numbering of the *Vulgate. The numbering of the Psalms in the Hebrew Bible is slightly different.

In speaking of the Messianic Psalms it is important to note that no single Psalm gives a total picture of the Messiah. But the combined picture offers an impressive

portrayal of the Messianic figure. Thus, Psalm 2 tells of
a king before whom all the kings and judges of the world
are called to bow in adoration; Psalm 21 describes a man
in great suffering, at whose story the nations shall return
to Yahweh; and Psalm 109 exultantly proclaims both the
kingship and the eternal priesthood of the Messiah.

PROVERBS:

The Hebrew term for a proverb is "Mashal", which
ordinarily means a short, concise saying, containing a
criticism of life or manners or character. The same word
may also be applied to a parable, allegory, or a similar
form of literature. The *Book of Proverbs* is, accordingly,
more than a collection of epigrams, or short sayings; in
fact, the literary forms and subject matter in this Book
are so miscellaneous that it is difficult to set them down
under any one heading. As noted earlier, Israel was a
latecomer in the field of sapiential writing. In Egypt
collections of wisdom texts were almost as old as the
Pyramids, while Mesopotamian wisdom literature looked
to the ancient land of Sumer as its place of origin. Until
about twenty years ago, practically nothing was known
about Sumerian wisdom. But, in recent years, the excavations of the buried cities of Sumer have brought a rich
harvest of clay tablets, some of which are older than 2000
B.C. Many of these tablets are still in the process of
publication and Sumerian scholars will be busy for many
years in the translation and interpretation of this valuable
material. When the picture is complete, we will have a
much better idea of the antiquity and range of wisdom
literature, and the extent to which the Israelite sage borrowed from the accumulated wisdom of the ancient Near
East.

Just as the whole Law has been attributed to Moses, and the entire *Book of Psalms* to David, so the whole *Book of Proverbs* is assigned to Solomon, whose reputation for wisdom was traditional in Israel. It is certain, of course, that not all of the Book, as it now stands, came from the pen of Solomon. But there is no justification for ruling out a Solomonic nucleus to the Book; we cannot discount the opinion that some of these sayings go back to the wise King who is known to have been a collector of proverbs. As many as nine distinct parts, of unequal length and importance, can be distinguished in the Book. Some of these parts are merely appendices to more substantial collections. The more important elements of the work can be grouped under five headings.

1.   (chaps. 1 to 9) This is the renowned "Praise of Wisdom" and consists of a series of exhortations to acquire that virtue above all else. It serves as a long Prologue to the entire Book, and its form is, throughout, poetical. Of particular interest to us is the personification of Wisdom, companion and counsellor of Yahweh from the beginning. It is by Wisdom that God operates in the world He created. Some interpreters have claimed that this personification of Wisdom opens up an entirely new horizon in Old Testament theology by teaching the eternal existence of a really distinct and divine person. According to this opinion, Wisdom would be identified with the Second Person of the Blessed Trinity. It seems more probable, however, that the poet-author intended the personification of Wisdom as a literary, artistic device. Parallels exist for this both in the Old Testament and in other ancient literature. On the other hand, the early Fathers of the Church and the Theologians have correctly

seen in this magnificent poem, with its vivid personification of Wisdom, the first intimation of and preparation for the great mystery of the Trinity.

2.   (chaps. 10 to 22:16) This collection is entitled "The Proverbs of Solomon", and contains not only religious maxims but counsels for practically every state in life. In these verses we meet all classes in Hebrew society, rich and poor, good and bad; but the pleasanter, more cheerful aspects of life are predominant.

3.   (chaps. 22:17 to 24:22) In 1924 the great Egyptologist, Adolph Erman, noted the close similarity between this section and the *Sayings of Amen-em-Opet,* preserved on an Egyptian papyrus which went back to the tenth century B.C. These Sayings are, in all probability, the source of the Hebrew collection. Such cultural interchange was quite common in the ancient Near East and is especially understandable when we recall that Egypt's influence extended for many centuries over the whole length of the Palestinian coast.

4.   (chaps. 25 to 29) The title of this collection informs us that these 128 proverbs are also Solomonic in their origin but were copied out by the men of Hezekiah, King of Judah.

5.   (chap. 31:10-31) This alphabetic poem, praising the valiant woman, is one of the best-known passages in the Old Testament. The Roman Liturgy uses the entire poem as the Epistle for the Mass of a Holy Woman Not a Martyr.

It is unwise, in fact impossible, to draw any systematic doctrine or theology from these collections, which vary so much among themselves and range over such a wide field of interest. Such systematizing would be too artificial, and false to the literary type with which we are dealing. Though many of the proverbs, at first sight, seem to be but expressions of worldly wisdom, closer scrutiny reveals a deep understanding of man as the creature of Yahweh and as the subject of His just rewards and punishments. Wisdom is a gift of God and a most precious treasure; above all, it is a virtue which is practical, directing men along the right way. And the characteristic teaching of *Proverbs* lies in the insight that the beginning of wisdom is the "fear of the Lord".

ECCLESIASTES:

The author of these reflections on the vanity of human life and ambitions is called "Qoheleth", son of David and king in Jerusalem. "Qoheleth" or "Preacher" is a name given to Solomon, whom Israelite tradition regarded not only as a teacher of wisdom, but as the first and outstanding representative of a special literary form—the sapiential writings. We know that Solomon did not write the present work; but beyond that, we have little positive information as to the author. It seems more probable that *Ecclesiastes* was written in Hebrew during the fourth century by a Jew who did not reside in Jerusalem but in the north of Palestine. It is difficult to determine precisely where the author lived but it is probable that he came from the Galilee area, or even closer to the Sea, from Tyre or Sidon. Strong Phoenician literary influences can be detected throughout the twelve chapters, strengthening the view that *Ecclesiastes* had a northern origin.

Authorship is only one of many problems in this very puzzling Book, which not only fails to mention even once the name of Yahweh, but says nothing about the Covenant, the Law, cult or Temple. Although the twelve chapters resist anything like neat classification, a few basic ideas run through the whole work. Among them we find the observation that man's restless ambitions are "vanity of vanities and a striving after wind"; also the advice to enjoy in moderation the gifts God has given to us. The final admonition is one which defines the one thing necessary for man: "Fear God, and keep His commandments".

The Preacher may often seem to paint the human scene in colors which are too sombre for our tastes, but it would be wrong to look upon him as just a pessimist, completely disillusioned with life and human effort. His faith in God is apparent at all times, and he recognizes an order in the world created by God. This keen observer saw only too well that men do violence to this order, and this accounts, perhaps, for the melancholy tone which runs through these reflections. The total picture would undoubtedly have been brighter had the author shared our clear revelation of immortality. But at this stage of revelation, life after death meant that existence in the shadowy land of *Sheol where there was "no work, nor device, nor knowledge, nor wisdom". We are still far from the certitudes of the future life and the joys of the beatific vision, all of which awaited later revelation. In this sense, the "confessions" of this sage were a product of his age, with all its limitations. God did not reveal everything at once. Still, *Ecclesiastes* is important, not for having found an answer to the mystery of human ambitions and frustrations, but for having brought the problem to the fore, and for having at least set us on the way to a solution.

"For God shall bring every work into the judgment concerning every hidden thing, whether it be good or whether it be evil." (ECCL. 12:14)

SONG OF SONGS:

There are many beautiful canticles in the Old Testament, such as the two Canticles of Moses (*Exodus* 15:1-18 and *Deut.* 32:1-43), and the moving Canticle of Anna (*I Sam.* 2:1-10). The expression "Song of Songs" is a Hebrew idiom denoting that this is the song or canticle *par excellence*. We have a familiar parallel in the phrase "Holy of Holies", denoting the most sacred part of the Temple. Jewish commentators have generally interpreted the *Song of Songs* as an allegory of Yahweh's love for His people, Israel. It was an easy transition for early Christian writers to go beyond this allegorical interpretation and extend it to Christ's love for His Church. In modern times interpretations have multiplied until there is little unanimity of opinion. Some see in the poems only profane, oriental love-songs, others are very anxious to relate the work to similar compositions in the literature of Egypt or Mesopotamia. While we may admit some superficial resemblance between the *Song of Songs* and non-Israelite literature, the soundest interpretation is that which places the work squarely in the literary and theological tradition of Israel itself. The imagery, the ideals, and the aspirations of the Book are thoroughly biblical, and perfectly consistent with the Old Testament world of ideas, as we know them from the sapiential and especially the prophetic writings. The marriage symbol as an expression of Yahweh's love for His wayward people was already well-known from *Hosea, Jeremiah*, and *Isaiah*; and this same symbol is made the basis of this work.

The two leading characters of the *Song of Songs* are Yahweh and the nation Israel, and they are personified as two lovers. On condition that we do not allow the allegorical interpretation to get out of hand by a fanciful exegesis of details, we are justified in seeing the allegorized love of Yahweh for His people as the general theme of the *Song of Songs*. Without excluding the possibility of other divisions, Father Robert, Professor of the Catholic Institute in Paris, has outlined the *Song of Songs* in the following manner:

Prologue: 1:2 to 4.
First Poem: 1:5 to 2:7.
Second Poem: 2:8 to 3:5.
Third Poem: 3:6 to 5:1.
Fourth Poem: 5:2 to 6:3.
Fifth Poem: 6:4 to 8:3.
Epilogue: 8:4 to 14.

The Canticle has always been a favorite with Christian mystics who have often expressed the rapture of their love in the language of this masterpiece. And the Liturgy has also borrowed its phrases to hymn the mutual love of Christ and His Mother.

BOOK OF WISDOM:

The Jewish communities living outside of Palestine after the Exile constituted what was known as the Diaspora. One of the largest of these groups had settled in Alexandria, the intellectual and scientific center of the Hellenistic world. There, one could study in the famous Library or, on the great boulevards, converse with the leading scholars of the day. Persecution of the Jews was apt to flare up at any moment, and it seems that one of these disturbances was the occasion of this Book, written by a pious and cultivated Jew. The date cannot be fixed with certainty, but the most likely is the first half of the first century before Christ.

The unknown author, writing under the name of Solomon, addressed his exhortation primarily to his fellow-Jews, urging them to seek Wisdom as the way to eternal life. The praise of Wisdom and its importance for man, whether king or pauper, are central themes in this gem of sapiential literature. Wisdom is the divine attribute constantly in the forefront of his thoughts. So realistically is it portrayed that some have seen in this Book a true personification of Wisdom, especially in a passage like 7:25-26. It is more probable, however, that the personification is a literary device, a poetic personification. But, just as in the case of *Proverbs,* there can be little doubt that this personification had its part in leading men to the mystery of the Trinity. At least such a personification helped to prepare the minds of men for the later, New Testament revelation of Christ and the Holy Spirit as two Persons distinct from the Father.

Besides the praise of Wisdom, the author warned his fellow-Jews against the blandishments of the pagans, and sought to strengthen them against what seemed like an imminent persecution. The dangers of idolatry were real in Alexandria. For example, its renowned Temple, the Serapeum, which was second only to the Roman Capitol in its splendor, opened its doors to all, including Jews. To rally their harassed spirits, the writer contrasted, in a passage of great power, the lot of the wicked and the just (chaps. 2 and 3).

In these chapters the hard-pressed, sorely tried Jew learned the good news that "God has made man for immortality". After death, the soul of the just man lived, not in the pale, shadowy reaches of Sheol, but a life of eternal happiness in the presence of God. This was the first time in the Old Testament that the doctrine of immortality had been taught clearly and unequivocally. From this time on, men had the important key to unlock the mystery of reward and punishment which tormented the Jewish soul for so many centuries. The alternatives of life and death now stood clearly before man, and it was in his power to choose. Humanity fell under two standards, the friends and the enemies of God, divisions which would persist throughout eternity. This revelation of personal immortality provided an ideal transition from the Old Covenant to the Mediator of the New, Jesus Christ, Son of God and eternal Wisdom.

The Book is divided into three main parts:

1.   (chaps. 1 to 5) Wisdom brings eternal life to the just and faithful man. The lot of the unjust and apostates is everlasting death.

2.   (chaps. 6 to 9) Wisdom's origin, nature, and activity are explained. Solomon's beautiful prayer for Wisdom (chap. 9) climaxes this part.

3.   (chaps. 10 to 19) Wisdom is described as operative in the sacred history of the Chosen People, from Adam to the Exodus. This meditation on Israel's past and the lessons drawn from it are a characteristic trait of post-exilic writing. Reflecting upon God's Providence manifested in the long history of Israel, these writers were not satisfied with a mere recitation of past events. They sought to disengage the meaning of that history, to go beyond the facts and discover the underlying principles. For that reason their narratives were more than chronicles; they gave us a theology of history which sought out the purposes of God.

The *Book of Wisdom* was never admitted into the Jewish Canon, and both Jews and Protestants class it among the Apocrypha. But it has, from the earliest times, enjoyed great prestige in the Catholic Church. Although we have not a single explicit citation of *Wisdom* in the New Testament, there is no doubt that both St. John and St. Paul were debtors to this Book in their Christological teaching (See *Coloss.* 1:15 ; *Heb.* 1:3 ; *John* 5:20). On St. John the influence is probably more profound. Whoever opens the pages of the Fourth Gospel will see in the Prologue how *Wisdom* has prepared the way for the theology of the Word made Flesh.

ECCLESIASTICUS:

The opening words "All wisdom comes from the Lord", places this Book in the Wisdom tradition. The Greek text of the Bible, known as the Septuagint, entitles the work, "Wisdom of Jesus, Son of Sirach". In English, the author is called simply "Ben Sira", or even "Sirach". St. Jerome tells us that the Book was called *Ecclesiasticus* among the Latins, and so it is entitled in the Vulgate translation.

Ben Sira was a sage of Jerusalem, a man of insight and learning who observed carefully the ever-shifting scenes of daily life enacted before him in the streets of old Jerusalem. Being a teacher as well as a scholar, Ben Sira set down his reflections and his accumulated wisdom in these maxims and essays which make up the longest Book of Jewish Wisdom Literature.

The date of composition is around 180 B.C., just before the outbreak of the Maccabean Revolt against the Seleucid oppressor. The translation was undertaken by the author's grandson, and completed around 130 B.C. For centuries the Hebrew text was lost to scholars. Then, in the last decade of the past century, a chance discovery of four manuscripts in a Genizah (storage place for worn-out manuscripts) of Old Cairo accounted for about two thirds of the Hebrew text of *Ecclesiasticus*. A fifth manuscript came to light in 1931. These five manuscripts provide a valuable check on the Greek translation.

In the Prologue the grandson of Ben Sira describes the labor he expended in putting the Hebrew original into the Greek, while he was a resident of Egypt. Many of the Jews resident in Egypt had forgotten their own language and knew only Greek, the common tongue of the Hellenistic world. Though the learned author did not write according to any fixed plan, we discern two major divisions, chapters 1 to 23, and 24 to 50. Each of these sections begins with a long eulogy of Wisdom.

Part I. (chaps. 1 to 23) These counsels of the wise teacher cover a vast field of conduct, from respect for parents to the proper use of wealth. He is vitally interested in the Law, the priesthood, and Temple service, but he also sees that sacrifice without a proper intention is not acceptable to God. Right conduct and personal holiness are demanded by God.

Part II. (chaps. 24 to 50) Personified Wisdom describes her divine origin and her part in the works of creation. Then follows a series of counsels on marriage, business transactions, friendship, education, good manners, and many other activities of daily life. The climax is the renowned "Praise of the Fathers of old" (chap. 44 to 50), a magnificent recapitulation of the deeds of Israel's heroes, men of piety and faith. The Book closes with a hymn of thanksgiving to God Who has been Savior, protector and helper of this venerable Master in Israel.

"I looked for the help of men, and there was none.
Then I remembered your mercy, O Lord,
And your work which has been from of old,
For You deliver those who wait for You,
And save them from the hand of their enemies."
(51:7-8)

* * * * * *

GLOSSARY

AB: The name of the fifth month of the Babylonian and Jewish calendar. It corresponded, approximately, to our month of August.

ADAR: The twelfth month of the Jewish year. The name was borrowed from the Babylonian calendar during the Exile.

ACHAEMENIAN: The name given to the Persian Empire of Cyrus the Great and his successors. The word is derived from Achaemenes, a Persian king of the seventh century, who gave his name to the whole Achaemenian Dynasty.

ALLEGORY: It is a literary form consisting of an extended comparison which is used to teach a moral or religious lesson. The comparison is based upon an extended series of metaphors, each with its appropriate meaning. Isaiah made use of allegory in chap. 5:1-7, comparing, by a sustained metaphor, Israel to a carefully tended vine. A Parable is also a comparison but, unlike the Allegory, each detail is not meant to have a particular application.

AMARNA AGE: That period in Egyptian history dominated by the Pharaoh Akh-en-Aton (1377-1360). At his capital, Tell el-Amarna, more than 350 letters were found, written on clay tablets. These letters were sent from Syria, Palestine, and Mesopotamia, to the Egyptian court. The tablets, discovered in 1887, are of great historical value for the light they shed on the Near East of that period.

APOCALYPTIC LITERATURE: A form of writing which consists in describing divine revelations usually given to some famous biblical character of the past (Adam, Noah, Henoch, etc.). These revelations, which always look to the future, are communicated in mysterious and symbolic language. Apocalyptic writing is later than Prophetic literature, and is especially popular in a time of crisis. Much of *Daniel* is apocalyptic.

APOCRYPHA: The Books, or parts of books, of the Old Testament, which were handed down in Greek, and were denied the rank of Holy Scripture in the Jewish Canon of Scripture. Protestants follow this Canon. Among Catholics these Books are called "Deuterocanonical".

The Council of Trent, in 1546, declared these Writings to be sacred and canonical. The books which Catholics call "Apocrypha" are not inspired and therefore not in the Bible.

APOLOGETICS: The systematic defense, through the light of natural reason, of the teachings of the Catholic Church.

ARAMAIC: A Semitic language which, as early as the eighth century B.C., became the international language of commerce and politics in the Near East. In Palestine it succeeded in replacing Hebrew as a living language. Our Lord and the Apostles spoke Aramaic.

ARCHAEOLOGY: The science which studies the life and culture of man as it is revealed through excavation. Biblical Archaeology is concerned with every discovery which can throw light on the biblical record.

BAAL: The king of the gods and the leader of the Canaanite pantheon. He was a storm-god and a giver of fertility. The word *ba'lu* means "lord, master".

BIBLICAL COMMISSION: Established by Pope Leo XIII in 1902, its membership is made up of Cardinals, assisted by Consultors from all parts of the world. Its duties are to direct and control the teaching of Sacred Scripture throughout the Catholic world. The Commission also has the right to confer academic degrees in Sacred Scripture.

CANON: The authoritative collection of sacred writings, recognized and received as inspired by the Catholic Church. The Catholic Canon of Scripture was solemnly defined in 1546 at the Council of Trent.

CARCHEMISH: A settlement located on the modern frontier between Turkey and Syria, at the western bend of the Euphrates. It was the site of one of the decisive battles of history (605 B.C.). The victory of Babylon over Egypt set the stage for the Babylonian Captivity of the Jews.

CODEX: An ancient book, made up of separate leaves fastened together. In antiquity it competed with, and finally supplanted, the papyrus roll, which was made by glueing papyrus sheets so as to form one long strip. In biblical times the roll was the common writing material (See *Luke* 4: 16-20).

UNCIAL CODEX: An ancient manuscript written in capital letters. These manuscripts are ordinarily of superior legibility and beauty. The "minuscule" is the opposite of the "uncial". The most important uncial codices of the Bible are:

A. *Codex Sinaiticus,* from the fourth century A.D., containing Old and New Testaments. Formerly at St. Catherine's Monastery on Mt. Sinai it is now in the possession of the British Museum.

B. *Codex Vaticanus,* from the fourth century A.D., with both Old and New Testaments. It is the property of the Vatican Library.

C. *Codex Alexandrinus,* from the fifth century A.D., with both Old and New Testaments. It is now in the British Museum.

All three of these codices are written on sheets of vellum, prepared from the skins of animals. They are written in Greek.

COVENANT: An agreement between two or more persons. In the Old Testament the word refers to the bond between Yahweh and Israel, which is the basis of Israel's religion. Christ came to establish a New Covenant which He sealed with His death on the Cross.

DAY OF YAHWEH: A great day of judgment in which the wicked will be punished, and holiness and peace will triumph. It is an eschatological (end of time) term. In the New Testament it is the Day on which Christ, as Judge, will come in the glory of the Father.

DEUTEROCANONICAL: The sacred books of either Old or New Testament about whose divine origin there had been some doubts. See CANON.

EXEGESIS: The science of correctly interpreting the text of the Bible. It comes from a Greek word meaning "to explain".

FEAST OF PURIM: It was instituted to celebrate the deliverance of the Jews from their mortal enemy, Haman. He had cast a "pur" (lot) to determine the day of the massacre of the Jews. The Feast is kept in the middle of the Jewish month of Adar, which ordinarily coincides with our month of February.

FEAST OF TABERNACLES: It is also called the "Feast of Booths". The Feast is kept in the autumn, at the end of the agricultural year. The booths, set up during the Feast, remind the Jewish people of the Exodus and their wanderings in the wilderness.

FEAST OF WEEKS: Sometimes it is called the "Feast of the Harvest". It is celebrated fifty days after Passover, and thus corresponds to the Christian Pentecost.

HANUKKAH: The Feast which celebrates the Purification and Rededication of the Temple by Judas Maccabeus. This took place in 165 B.C. The Hebrew word *hanukkah* means "dedication". The Feast is celebrated in the Jewish month of Chislev, which corresponds approximately with our December.

HASMONEAN HOUSE: Commonly used to designate the ruling family of the Maccabean Age, from Mattathias to Herod the Great. The family name of Mattathias was probably "Hashmonay".

HELLENISM: The pursuit of Greek culture and the cultivation of the Greek language by people who were non-Greeks. The Hellenistic Rule in the Near East extends from the victory of Alexander the Great at the Battle of Issus (333 B.C.) to the Conquest of Palestine by Pompey (63 B.C.).

HIGHER CRITICISM: The study of the Bible from a literary and historical viewpoint. It is to be distinguished from Lower (textual) Criticism which aims to reproduce, as far as possible, the text as it came from the original author.

INERRANCY: That quality of Sacred Scripture by which the assertions of its authors are free of all error. Inerrancy is a necessary consequence of inspiration.

INSPIRATION: The supernatural impulse by which God has moved the human author to write in such a way that God is the principal author. The human writer is an instrumental cause, but also a true author.

LEVIRATE LAW: If a man died childless, the Mosaic Law obliged the brother of the deceased to marry the widow. In this way children were raised up in the name of the first man, and the dead man's name did not perish in Israel. (*Deut.* 25: 5 ff.)

MARCION: He was a heretic of the second century who rejected the entire Old Testament and parts of the New Testament, in his canon of Sacred Scripture.

MARI: An ancient city on the banks of the Middle Euphrates, discovered in 1933 and excavated by French archaeologists. The City flourished in the time of Hammurabi (1728-1686). The royal archives, consisting of over tweny thousand tablets, are now in the process of publication.

MER-NE-PTAH: He was Pharaoh of Egypt in the Imperial Era. He set up the famous "Israel Stele" on which he inscribed his Hymn of Victory, about 1220 B.C. The Stele is important for determining the time when Israel entered the land of Canaan.

NIPPUR: A sacred City of the Sumerians, and a religious center of the god En-lil, "Lord of the Storm". The valuable Sumerian literature found at the site is now in the Museums of Istanbul and the University of Pennsylvania.

NUZU: An ancient site in eastern Mesopotamia, near modern Kirkuk, Iraq. Since the first excavations in 1925, numerous tablets from this mound have been published, giving us a better understanding of the Patriarchal Age.

PAPYRUS: A tall plant which flourishes along the marshes of the Nile. It was used extensively as writing material in the ancient world. Many papyrus texts have been preserved for centuries in Egypt because of the dry climate which prevails.

PARABLE: A popular story told to illustrate a moral or religious truth. Parables formed an important part of our Lord's teaching. The parables of the Good Shepherd, the Unjust Steward, and the Good Samaritan, may be cited as examples. See ALLEGORY.

PARALLELISM: This is a characteristic quality of Hebrew and other Semitic poetry. It consists in balancing the two equal parts of a single verse. The second half of the verse may express the same idea as the first half (synonymous parallelism), or the exact opposite (antithetic parallelism). Examples of this stylistic quality abound in the *Psalms* and *Proverbs*.

PASSOVER: This is the most solemn Jewish festival of the year; it celebrates their deliverance from Egypt, as narrated in *Exodus*. The festival begins on the 14th of Nisan (usually in the month of April) with the eating of the Paschal Lamb, and continues for seven days. The Passion of our Lord took place during the Feast of the Passover (Pasch) in Jerusalem.

PHARISEE: The word is derived from Hebrew and means "to separate". The Pharisee was a member of a religious party which probably originated at the time that Hellenism threatened Judaism in Palestine. The religious life of a Pharisee centered in the Law and its interpretation. The danger of excessive legalism was always present.

POST-EXILIC: The Babylonian Exile, 587-538, marked a turning-point in the history of Israel. Events, institutions, and writings which belong to the period after the Return to Palestine in 538, are called "post-Exilic".

RAMSES II: (1290-1224) This Pharaoh of the Nineteenth Dynasty was famous for the massive monuments with which he covered Egypt. Biblical tradition connects the oppression of the Israelites with the building of two of his cities in the Nile Delta, Pithom and Ramses.

RAS SHAMRA: See "UGARIT".

REDACTION: A redactor is one who prepares or edits literary material for publication. The finished product is a redaction. In a redaction we sometimes find rearrangement, revision, or adaptation of the original material.

SADDUCEES: A Jewish religious party which was recruited largely from the priestly and aristocratic class. The Pharisees, on the contrary, drew largely from the mass of the populace. Both parties, though opposed to one another on specific points of theology, appear together in the New Testament as adversaries of our Lord.

SAPIENTIAL LITERATURE: These are writings which sought to study the nature of things and their relation to man and God. Though much of this literature was the product of observation and experience, wisdom was nevertheless a gift of God and was given only to the man who feared God. Sapiential is derived from the Latin word "sapiens", meaning "wise".

SATRAPY: A title used during the Persian period to denote a province under the control and protection of the King of Persia. The authorized representative of the king was called a "satrap" or "protector" of the land.

SELEUCID: This name was given to the succession of Syrian kings who controlled Jerusalem from 198 B.C. until the time of the Maccabean struggle in 175 B.C. The founder of the Dynasty was Seleucus I, who established Seleucid rule over Syria, Mesopotamia, Persia, and the southern part of Asia Minor. The Dynasty was Hellenistic in its culture.

SEPTUAGINT: This Greek work is the best known and most important translation of the Old Testament. The word "Septuagint" means "seventy", and recalls the legend that seventy men composed the board of translators. The Septuagint translation was practically complete by the end of the second century B.C.

SHEOL: According to Old Testament ideas of the future life Sheol was the place where the spirits of the dead continued to exist. It was a place below the earth, shadowy and depressing. Another name for it was "the Pit".

STELE: (or "stela") is a Greek word denoting an erect stone slab which is used for a memorial inscription. The tombstone is a very common example of the Stele. In ancient times, victories were often recorded on a stele.

SUMER: The ancient name for the southern part of Babylonia. It was the site of the earliest civilization in the Near East. The chief cities of Sumer were Nippur, Lagash and Ur.

THEOPHANY: A manifestation or appearance of God to man. This could be either in person, as at Sinai, or by means of the Angel of the Lord.

TYPOLOGY: The science of determining the typical sense in the Old Testament. God, the principal author of Scripture, has intended that certain persons, institutions or things should signify and point ahead to some person, institution or thing in the New Testament. The Paschal Lamb is a type of Christ, as the Manna is a type of the Holy Eucharist.

UGARIT: This ancient Canaanite city on the eastern shore of the Mediterranean is more commonly known as Ras Shamra (fennel head). Discovered in 1928, excavations were begun the following year by a French archaeological expedition and are still in progress. The most important find at Ras Shamra has been the ancient Canaanite literature which has greatly aided our understanding of many biblical passages.

VULGATE: This is St. Jerome's Latin version of the Bible, completed in 405 A.D. It derives its name from the Latin word *vulgare* "to publish, make common, spread abroad". The translation, a landmark of Christian latinity, became the official Bible of the Church in the West, and was the first book to be printed on the Gutenberg Press.

WELLHAUSEN: Julius Wellhausen (1844-1918) was a German biblical scholar and orientalist. He is best known for his defense and popularization of the Documentary Hypothesis as applied to the first six books of the Bible. His false theological and historical suppositions have rendered many of his conclusions obsolete.

ZION: The southeast hill of Jerusalem which was captured by David from the native Jebusites and renamed the "City of David". Zion is sometimes used in the Old Testament to signify all of Jerusalem. It may also denote that spiritual Jerusalem which is a symbol of the true Church.

A GUIDE TO PRONUNCIATION

ACHAEMENIAN
(ah-kay-méan-ian)

ADAR (ah-dár)

AHASUERUS (a-ha-zoo-ér-us)

AHAZ (áy-haz)

AKH-EN-ATON
(ack-en-áh-ton)

AMALEKITES (ah-mál-eh-kites)

AMEN-EM-OPET
(amen-em-óh-pet)

ANATOTH (án-a-toth)

ANTIOCHUS (an-tíe-o-cuss)

ASAPH (áy-saf)

ATHALIAH (ath-ah-ly'e-ah)

BAAL (báy-al)

BALAAM (báy-lam)

BALAC (báy-lak)

BARUCH (bár-uk)

BETHULIA (beth-óo-lee-ah)

BOAZ (bóh-as)

CANAAN (káy-nan)

CARCHEMISH (kár-kay-mish)

CHEBAR (káy-bar)

DEPHKAH (déf-kah)

DEUTERONOMY
(due-ter-ón-oh-me)

DIASPORA (die-áss-po-rah)

ECCLESIASTES
(e-klee-zee-áss-teez)

ECCLESIASTICUS
(e-klee-zee-áss-ti-kuss)

EDOM (ée-dum)

ELEAZAR (el-ee-áy-zar)

ELIHU (eh-ly'e-hue)

ELIJAH (ee-ly'e-jah)

ELIMELECH (eh-li'm-e-leck)

EPHRAIM (éf-rah-im)

EPIPHANES (eh-píf-fah-neez)

ESDRAELON (ez-dra-áy-lon)

EXODUS (ék-so-duss)

EZEKIEL (e-zéek-ee-el)

EZION-GEBER
(áy-zee-on géb-er)

GENESIS (jén-e-sis)

GENIZAH (ge-née-zah)

GIDEON (gíd-ee-un)

GILBOA (gil-bó-ah)

GLUECK (glick)

HABAKKUK (háb-ah-cook)

HAGGAI (hág-eye)

HAMAN (háy-man)

HAMMURABI
(ham-moo-ráh-bee)

HANUKKAH (hah-núk-kah)

HASMONEAN (haz-mo-née-an)

HOSEA (hoe-záy-ah)

HYKSOS (hík-sauce)

ISAIAH (eye-záy-ah)

JEHOIACHIN (jeh-hóy-ah-kin)

JEREMIAH (jer-eh-my'-ah)

JEROBOAM (jer-oh-bó-am)

JOSHUA (jósh-you-ah)

JOSIAH (joe-cy'-ah)

LACHISH (láy-kish)

LEVITICUS (leh-vít-i-cuss)

MACCABEES (máck-ah-bees)

MALACHI (mál-ah-ky)

MARI (máh-ree)
MASHAL (mah-shál)
MEGIDDO (meg-gi'd-doe)
MER-NE-PTAH
   (mare-nép-tah)
MERODACH (meh-róe-dak)
MICAH (my'-kah)
MORDECAI (mór-de-kai)

NAHUM (náy-hum)
NAOMI (nay-óh-mee)
NEBUCHADNEZZAR
   (ne-byu-khad-néz-zar)
NEHEMIAH (nee-he-my'-ah)
NICANOR (nee-káy-nor)
NIPPUR (níp-poor)
NUZU (nóo-zoo)

OBADIAH (oh-ba-díe-ah)

PARALIPOMENON
   (pa-ra-li-póm-en-on)
PENTATEUCH (pén-tah-tyuk)
PHARAOH (fáir-oh)
POMPEY (póm-pee)

QOHELETH (ko-hél-eth)

RAHAB (ráy-hab)
RAMSES (rám-sees)

SAMARIA (sah-máre-ee-ah)
SATRAPY (sáy-trap-ee)
SEIR (sáy-ir)

SELEUCID (se-lóo-sid)
SENNACHERIB (sen-nák-er-ib)
SEPHER TEHILLIM
   (sáy-fer teh-hil-léem)
SEPTUAGINT (sép-tu-ah-jint)
SERABIT EL-KHADEM
   (sér-ah-bit el-káh-dem)
SHEAR YASHUB
   (shée-ar-yáh-shoob)
SHEOL (shé-ole)
SHEPHELAH (sheh-fáy-lah)
SHISHAK (shy'-shak)
SIRACH (sére-ak)
STELE (stéel-ee)
SUMER (sóo-mer)

TELL ABIB (tell-ah-béeb)
TIGLATH PILESER
   (tíg-lath pie-lée-zer)

UGARIT (yóu-gah-rit)
UZZIAH (uz-zy'e-ah)

XERXES (zérk-sees)

YAHWEH (yáh-way)

ZECHARIAH (zek-ah-ry'e-ah)
ZEDEKIAH (zed-eh-ky'e-ah)
ZEPHANIAH (zef-an-éye-ah)
ZERUBBABEL
   (zer-óob-bah-bell)
ZION (zái-on)

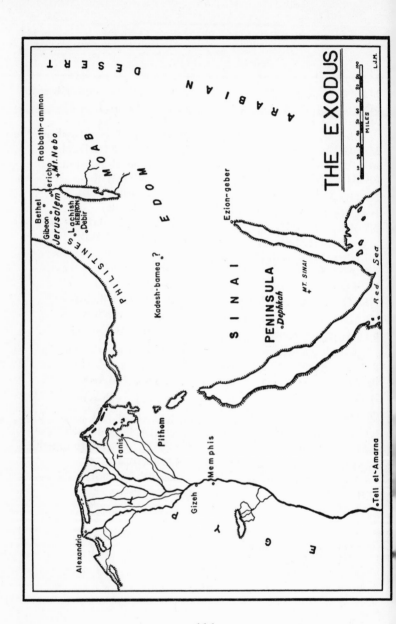

THE EXODUS

MILES

L.J.M.

116

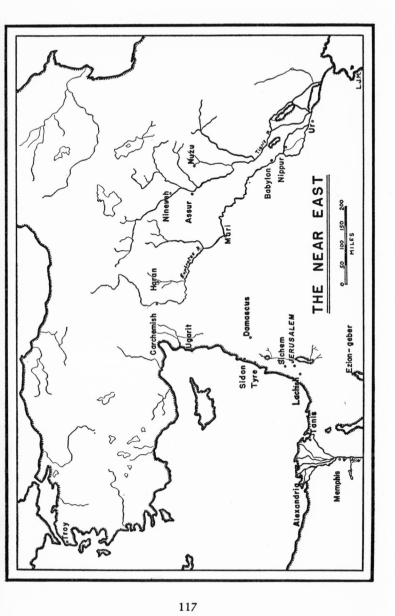

THE NEAR EAST

0 50 100 150 200
MILES

Troy

Alexandria

Memphis

Tanis

Sidon
Tyre
Lachish
Sichem
JERUSALEM
Ezion-geber

Damascus

Ugarit

Carchemish

Haran

Nineveh
Assur
Mari
Babylon
Nippur
Nuzu
Ur

L.J.M.

117

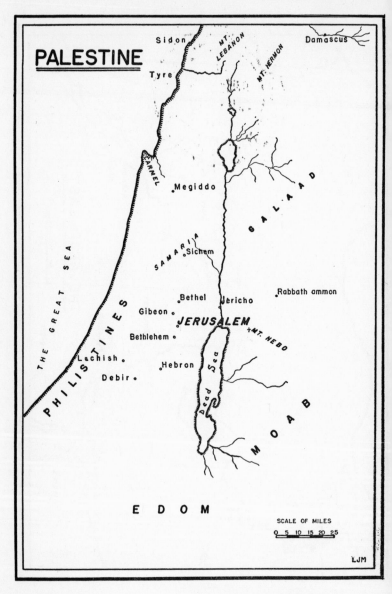

PALESTINE

Sidon

MT. LEBANON

Damascus

Tyre

MT. HERMON

CARMEL

• Megiddo

GALAAD

SAMARIA

THE GREAT SEA

• Sichem

• Bethel

• Rabbath ammon

Gibeon •

Jericho

JERUSALEM

PHILISTINES

Bethlehem •

• MT. NEBO

Lachish •

Dead Sea

Debir •

• Hebron

MOAB

EDOM

SCALE OF MILES

0 5 10 15 20 25

LJM